SE25 9A

# ECONOMIC CHOICE UNDER UNCERTAINTY

This book is dedicated with gratitude to
E.L. FELL
former Senior Classics and Economics master
at Calday Grange Grammar School, West Kirby:
an outstanding teacher who first introduced me
to the delights of Economic Theory.

# Economic Choice Under Uncertainty
## *A Perspective Theory Approach*

J.L. Ford
*Professor of Economics*
*University of Birmingham*

**EDWARD ELGAR**

Published by
Edward Elgar Publishing Ltd
Gower House
Croft Road
Aldershot
Hants GU11 3HR
England

**British Library Cataloguing in Publication Data**

Ford, J.L.
    Economic choice under uncertainty: a
    perspective theory approach.
    1. Economics—Decision making
    2. Uncertainty
    I. Title
    330    HB199

ISBN 1 85278 006 1

Typeset in Great Britain by
Guildford Graphics Limited, Petworth, West Sussex.
Printed and bound in Great Britain by
Billing and Sons Limited, Worcester.

# Contents

*Cur hane tibi, rector Olympi,*
*Sollicitis visum mortalibus addere curam,*
*Noscant venturas ut dira per omnia clades?*
*Sit subitum quodcunque paras, sit caeca futuri*
*Mens hominum fati, liceat sperare timenti.*

Lucan; quoted in Michel Eyquem de Montaigne's 'Of Prognostications' published in Volume 1 of his *Essais*.

# Preface

This book is concerned with choice under uncertainty. That knowledge cannot be gained before its time is a common notion, a platitude, for everyman. But so much of economic analysis involving decision either at the individual level or by the policy-maker for the macroeconomy has been conducted in the context of full information. However, in recent years manifold attempts have been made to move economics out of the sterility in which it became engulfed by ignoring uncertainty. Yet, in terms of decision-making by individual agents with limited knowledge, the conceptual paradigms propounded have been predicated upon the premise that lack of knowledge can be represented by a probability distribution for the potential outcomes that might ensue from a particular action-choice. The condition which renders the reliance on such a distribution for choice a meaningful one amounts to the individual's being able to sample the distribution continually; therefore, *reductio ad absurdum*, as it were, he is confronted not by ignorance, but by knowledge. Such, indeed, would be the view of George Shackle and probably also of Frank Knight – those stalwart campaigners against the confusion between risk and uncertainty.

The most prevalent conceptual framework in the literature concerned with individual choice under limited information is that of the Expected Utility Theory. Based, as it is, on the application of the probability calculus to the selection of the best out of a range of action-choices, with unknown consequences, it is a theory really of decision-taking under risk. The theory still dominates the literature despite the fact that it has been shown consistently, and continuously, over the past thirty years, to be refuted by numerous laboratory experiments. Those experiments, which have been undertaken by psychologists as well as economists, were designed to evaluate the efficacy of the axiomatic foundations of Expected Utility Theory, and to examine the truth of the Expected Utility Theorem, which is the guide-to-action emanating from the theory.

Two alternative theories, however, have recently been proposed: Prospect Theory and Regret Theory. Both of these were formulated as deliberate attempts to account for the phenomena observed in most laboratory experiments on choice over risky prospects (largely lotteries or bets). They are *ex post facto* theories.

So, *ex definitione,* they do, as it were, fit some of the facts related to choice over bets. However, both theories postulate a choice-index that is a weighted value of outcomes in the competing prospects offered by the alternative action-choices. Prospect Theory comes as close as is possible to advocating the weighting process or, as it is called, 'averaging process', embodied in the Expected Utility Theorem. Regret Theory is further removed from the Expected Utility Theorem, but it employs a kind of expected utility index to rank choices or strategies. Both theories are founded on probability as the 'uncertainty'-variable. Also, to date, both theories have been applied only to the choice over simple lotteries. Neither has been developed for application to more complex choices and to choices in a wider economic context, such as financial portfolio selection, investment in machinery or consumption-saving allocation. Furthermore, Regret Theory is not supported by every laboratory experiment.

In this monograph I propose and formalize a new approach called Perspective Theory, with which choices over prospects with unknown outcomes can be explicated. In addition, an alternative uncertainty-measure to objective or subjective probability, namely, a degree of belief, which is axiomatized, is propounded. Perspective Theory is formulated either in terms of that uncertainty-variable or of probability.

The only other theory that has been developed which does not rely on probability being the uncertainty-measure is the theory advocated by George Shackle, which is based on the concept of potential-surprise. My contention is that my degree of belief index does not suffer from the problems associated with Shackle's concept. Furthermore, although the formal structure of Perspective Theory has similarities with that advanced by Shackle, it differs from his, in so far as it offers the possibility of application to portfolio selection, and it can explain choice over lotteries which his, *ex definitione,* cannot since it excludes the use of probability as an uncertainty-variable. It must be conceded that individuals are given the choice over probability distributions in particular contexts (for example, of lottery tickets or bets). A theory of decision-making under incomplete information must be able to explain behaviour in those kinds of circumstances.

Besides having an affinity with Shackle over the illogicality of using probability as an uncertainty-variable in particular contexts, the formal apparatus of Perspective Theory does employ Shacklesque concepts. Nevertheless, they are only Shacklesque not Shacklean, as it were: in my model concepts have different roles to play when compared with those in Shackle's schema.

However, it has to be said that, when the ideas behind Perspective

Theory were developed more rigorously, they produced a theory that was much nearer to Shackle's view of the world than was the case initially. The prototype model produced a theory that was ostensibly radically different from his. The final version does have features in common with Shackle's theory. Indeed, it is possible to regard the complete version as removing the inconsistencies from, and filling in the lacunae in, Shackle's schema which I pointed out in *Choice, Expectation and Uncertainty* (Ford 1983), in a different way from that which I advocated in the model constructed in Chapter 5 of that book.

The ideas expressed in this book are simple, yet I hope elemental as well. They were first thought of when I had the pleasure to be Visiting Professor at the University of California, Los Angeles, in autumn 1969: as one of my duties, I gave postgraduate lectures in Economic Theory. I lectured on uncertainty in economics and there began my *Choice, Expectation and Uncertainty* book, which gave me the ideas for Perspective Theory. A further impetus to the development of the theory was a seminar I gave on Portfolio Selection and Choice Indices at the University of Liverpool in March 1976.

Several colleagues at Birmingham and elsewhere have done me the kindness of reading the first draft of this book. I have benefited enormously from their general comments about the organization of the material and from the specific points of detail they raised concerning Perspective Theory itself. Their support has been most encouraging; and although I have not felt able to incorporate all of their suggestions I hope that they will not be too disappointed with the revisions I have made.

I would, in particular, like to extend my thanks to: Charles Carter, David Dickinson, Michael Driscoll, John Hey, Mark Machina, Chris McKenna and Walter Krelle. I must also make a special mention of George Shackle, my mentor now for many years. Failing eyesight has prevented his providing me with all the detailed comments he has usually done: but, as always, his support and enthusiasm for what I have been attempting has been a rich reward in itself.

The list of acknowledgements would not be complete without my saying 'thank you' to Sally Berry, Marilyn Mansell and Chris Reynolds for the excellent way that they have coped with the daunting task of dealing with my untidy manuscripts and unfathomable handwriting. In that regard, a 'thank you' seems inadequate. Finally, I would like to express my gratitude to Ralph Bailey for providing the computer simulation results reported in Chapter 6, and for his elegant re-statement of the Appendix to that chapter.

J.L. Ford
October 1986

# PART I
# EXPECTED UTILITY THEORY:
# THEORETICAL AND EMPIRICAL OVERVIEW

# 1 Decision Criteria Under Uncertainty: Expected Utility and All That: A Summary of Alternatives

Ever since the pioneering work of Von Neumann and Morgenstern (1944, 1947) formalized the Expected Utility framework of Bernouilli (1738), Expected Utility and its corollary, the Expected Utility Theorem, have dominated the economics literature on choice under uncertainty. The reasons for its dominance cannot be expressed more succinctly or eloquently than by Mark Machina:

> As an approach to the theory of individual behaviour towards risk, the expected utility model is characterised by the simplicity and normative appeal of its axioms, the familiarity of the notions it employs (utility functions and mathematical expectation), the elegance of its characterisations of various types of behaviour in terms of properties of the utility function (risk aversion by concavity, the degree of risk aversion by the Arrow–Pratt measure, etc.), and the large number of results it has produced. It is thus not surprising that most current theoretical research in the economics of uncertainty, as well as virtually all applied work in the field (eg optimal trade, investment or search under uncertainty), is undertaken in the expected utility framework (Machina 1982: 277–8).

He makes it clear that he expects it to remain so in the future.

The model advanced by Von Neumann and Morgenstern was as similar as it could be to the celebrated Hicks–Allen (1934) formalization of the Paretian approach to choice under certainty. It was, therefore, readily understood by economists and viewed as dovetailing with orthodox methodology. Its axioms, like those of consumer theory, were simple and intuitively appealing as Machina suggested. They enabled many phenomena to be explained from very little, as it were.

The axioms stated how an individual economic agent should choose one 'gamble'; that is, over strategies (be they the choice of real investment, portfolios, or 'real' gambles such as lottery tickets or whatever) where the outcomes of any adopted strategy could not be known in advance. The strategies, or courses of action, would possess a probability distribution (continuous or discrete); so for example, in the case of a discrete probability density function, the various alternative outcomes from a given choice of action would have stated probabilities of occurrence attached to them. By virtue of the fact that the outcomes possess probability density functions, the probabilities over all outcomes for any specific course of action must sum to unity. If it is assumed that the outcomes are monetary values $(x_i)$ and the probability of any $x_i$ is represented by $\pi_i$, then a course of action, a 'gamble', would consist of a set of $(x_i, \pi_i)$; a 'certainty' would be the element $(x_i, 1)$ and a Bernouillian choice set would be $[(x_i, \pi_i), (x_j, 1 - \pi_i)]$.

The axioms of the Expected Utility Theory enable each $x_i$ in a choice or gamble to be represented by a 'utility' number $(U_i)$ and the choice or gamble *per se* to be encapsulated in an index equal to $\Sigma U_i \pi_i$, namely by its expected utility. The axioms demonstrate that if an individual has a preference for gamble $A$ over gamble $B$, the expected utility of $A$ must exceed that of $B$, and vice versa, so that the expected utility of $A$ will exceed that of $B$, if and only if the individual prefers gamble $A$ to gamble $B$. Thus, the axioms that are related to preferences over gambles produce choice that reflects preferences. There are several ways in which the axioms of the Expected Utility Theory can be presented; one such method is given in the Appendix to this chapter.

The Expected Utility Theorem is easy to comprehend and, more importantly, easy to apply to numerous decision-taking situations in Economics (and other areas). To 'crank the handle' and apply the theorem to the analysis of the optimum choice of portfolio, machinery, of labour search ... is relatively straightforward, and it produces tractable, econometrically testable, behavioural results. So it has inevitably had wide coverage in the literature. However as Machina has also remarked:

> Nevertheless, the expected utility hypothesis is still a particular hypothesis concerning individual preferences over alternative probability distributions over wealth (we may substitute 'outcomes') ... it became generally recognised that expected utility depended crucially on the empirical validity of the so-called 'independence axiom' ...
>
> The high normative appeal of the independence axiom has been widely (although not universally) acknowledged. However, the evidence concerning its *descriptive* validity is not quite as favourable ...
>
> In addition, a large amount of research on the validity of the expected utility model has appeared in the psychology literature (Machina 1982: 227–8).

Indeed, the empirical evidence assessing the truth of the axioms of Expected Utility Theory and of its predictions about behaviour under uncertainty, embodied in the Expected Utility Theorem, is now extensive by any standard. It is almost all unfavourable to the theory and its theorem. However, for the most part, as will be seen here and in Chapter 7, that negative empirical evidence has had very little impact on the use of, and the faith in, the Expected Utility Theorem. Where attempts have been made to accommodate the empirical evidence, they have resulted in slight amendments to the letter rather than to the spirit of Expected Utility Theory.

Within less than a decade of its appearance the Expected Utility Theory was being investigated empirically. The empirical tests were carried out predominantly by psychologists and consisted of laboratory experiments on the verisimilitude of the Expected Utility Theorem as a guide to choice. The experiments, to make the point more poignantly, were exercises given to small numbers (in some cases extremely small numbers of no more than a handful) of willing subjects, usually students, and were of a gambling/lottery ticket format, consisting, therefore, of choices that the participants had to make between alternatives that were composed of (usually) monetary outcomes and attached probabilities of occurrence. No econometric testing of the predictions for, say, the portfolio behaviour of individuals, or individual units such as financial institutions, was undertaken in the early days of the empirical assessment of Expected Utility Theorem. Subjects also were not given choices that (except in the very limiting way that lottery tickets capture the spirit of this) embraced asset choice, the choice of capital equipment or machinery that should be purchased, and so on; the lottery ticket paradigm has very limited economic application, only tangentially touching on asset choice and, tacitly, on the attitudes to the purchase of insurance.

As attempts to test rules of how decision-making is formulated by individuals, the early tests (*see* Mosteller and Magee 1951; Preston and Baratta 1948; and Edwards 1953, 1954a, 1954b, 1955) and their successors have had a limited perspective. The most notable limitation perhaps has been that they have presented subjects with choices over probability distribution and so-called objective probability distribution at that. In other words, those playing the role of decision-maker are given the choices that are open to them in an 'uncertain' world, and the information about that 'uncertainty' is cast entirely in terms of the (objective) probability of occurrence of the various (monetary) items that constitute each particular gamble or lottery.

The earliest tests of the Expected Utility Theorem were designed to judge whether or not the predictions of that theorem were true. The most obvious point to start such a potentially difficult inquiry was to use the controlled experiment approach of psychologists on simple lottery tickets or bets. Expected Utility Theory and its corollary, Expected Utility Theorem, must be consistent with individual choices over gambles; its veracity rests upon more than that, but in terms of Friedman's (1953) much-disputed methodological precepts (*see* Simon 1963; and Samuelson 1963) it must be successful in predicting behaviour in true gambling situations as one element, as it were, in the set of all feasible situations of choice under 'uncertainty'.

Even most, but not all, of the early studies of the Expected Utility Theorem in the above experimental context found that behaviour was not consistent with the theorem. This was the case even with the researches of Ward Edwards, which were arguably the most comprehensive and fastidious researches. He devised bets that were not straight lottery tickets and where subjective probability was allowed for as an alternative 'weight of evidence' variable to objective probability (*see*, especially, Edwards 1955). Over the years the evidence from tests of Expected Utility Theory over lottery selection has almost overwhelmingly been a refutation of the theory. The most thorough experimental data that have been generated in recent years have come from the efforts of Kahneman and Tversky (1973, 1979) and to a lesser extent from those of Kunreuther *et al.* (1978).

The major finding is that the Expected Utility Theory is not satisfied empirically and that the reason for this is that the axioms, behavioural assumptions, of the Expected Utility Theory model formulated by Von Neumann and Morgenstern are themselves refuted empirically. Choices over gambles or bets are made by the participants in the experiments which are inconsistent with the Expected Utility Theorem: that is, in one situation, say, gamble $A$ is chosen in preference to gamble $B$; in another, gamble $C$ is chosen over gamble $D$. Yet if the choice of gamble $A$ over gamble $B$ follows from the individual decision-taker's having maximized his Expected Utility from exercising that choice, the experiments are designed to demonstrate that $D$ should be preferred to $C$. The two choices are inconsistent with each other.

Comments on the range of empirical evidence will be made in Chapter 2, where there will also be details of some of the latest evidence available, namely, that produced by Kahneman and Tversky (1979).

The Expected Utility Theorem has also come under attack for other reasons, which are pseudo-empirical, in that they are based on the view that the Expected Utility paradigm is far too sophisticated a paradigm for the human mind to embrace. Such is the opinion of Herbert Simon, one of the staunchest and most vehement critics of the Expected Utility approach. Thus, in his Nobel Lecture (1979) he argued:

However, a strong positive case for replacing the classical theory by a model of bounded rationality begins to emerge when we examine situations involving decision-making under uncertainty and imperfect competition. These situations the classical theory was never designed to handle, and has never handled satisfactorily. Statistical-decision theory employing the idea of subjective, expected utility, on the one hand, and game theory, on the other, have contributed enormous conceptual clarification to these kinds of situations without providing satisfactory descriptions of actual human behaviour, or even, for most cases, normative theories that are actually usable in the face of the limited computational powers of men and computers (Simon 1979: 497–8).

In his Harry Camp Memorial Lectures (1982) he is more forthright, providing a pellucid, succinct, summary of the more lengthy arguments he gave in Simon (1979):

The SEU (Subjective-Expected Utility) model assumes that the decision-maker contemplates, in one comprehensive view, everything that lies before him. He understands the range of alternative choices open to him, not only at the moment but over the whole panorama of the future. He understands the consequences of each of the available choice strategies, at least up to the point of being able to assign a joint probability distribution to future states of the world. He has reconciled or balanced all his conflicting partial values and synthesized them into a single utility function that orders, by his preference for them, all these future states of the world. The SEU model finesses completely the origins of the values that enter into the utility function; they are simply there, already organized to express consistent preferences among all alternative futures that may be presented for choice. The SEU model finesses just as completely the processes for ascertaining the facts of the present and future states of the world. At best, the model tells us how to reason about fact and value premises; it says nothing about where they come from. When these assumptions are stated explicitly, it becomes obvious that SEU theory has never been applied, and can never be applied – with or without the largest computers – in the real world . . .
    The evidence, much of which has been assembled . . . by Amos Tversky and his colleagues, leaves no doubt whatever that human behaviour in these choice situations . . . departs widely from the prescriptions of SEU theory . . . I have already suggested what the principal reason is for this departure. It is that human beings have neither the facts nor the consistent structure of values nor the reasoning power at their disposal that would be required, even in these relatively simple situations, to apply SEU principles (Simon 1982: 13–17).

Arguments that theoretical models of either micro or macro behaviour are otiose, because they proffer models that assume economic agents to formulate their decisions in a formal, rigorous fashion that requires a high level of analytical and technical expertise, have only been advanced infrequently in the literature. They have usually been countered with great spirit and determination by arguments that are of the genre, 'the assumptions of the theory do not matter, all that is germane is the veracity of its predictions', or 'economic agents are not regarded as composing in their minds the formal apparatus that the axioms imply, rather they are to be envisaged as acting *as if* they did so, behaving in accordance with the hypothesis that is a corollary of the axioms.' Alternatively, the view is propounded that the axioms hold because they describe rational behaviour and so hold naturally, by the arguments of metatheory. The models of rational behaviour are unchallengeable, natural, phenomena and as such are irrefutable.

Those who champion the notion that economic agents consistently act rationally harness their support from either camp; and many do so accepting the line of argument advanced by Jacques Dreze, who has contributed himself so much to the study of 'uncertainty' in economics:

> A consistent decision-maker is assumed always to be able to compare (transitively) the attractiveness of acts, or hypothetical acts and of consequences as well as the likelihood of events. These requirements are minimal, in the sense that no consistency of behaviour may be expected if any one of them is violated: but they are very strong, in the sense that all kinds of comparisons are assumed possible, many of which may be quite remote from the range of experience of the decision-maker. This is also the reason why the axioms have more normative appeal than descriptive realism; few people would insist on maintaining, consciously, choices that violate them, but their spontaneous behaviour may frequently fail to display such rigorous consistency (Dreze 1974: 11).

Unless we are prepared to invoke the metapostulate that rational choice is part of the universe and it is formulated according to the Von Neumann–Morgenstern axioms, it will not follow that the Expected Utility Theory is sacrosanct. Rational, consistent choice under uncertainty could be both explained and accounted for by an alternative schema. As has been seen, Mark Machina, the most elegant champion of Expected Utility Theory – certainly of its expectation principle – does not dissent from that viewpoint.

Herbert Simon has drawn attention to the supposition that in utilizing the Expected Utility Theorem the individual decision-maker has available an exhaustive set of probabilities concerning the outcomes promised by any course of action. Furthermore, the Expected Utility Theorem is predicated on the notion that utilities of outcomes are weighted by their probability of occurrence. That expectation principle means that an averaging concept is being used: outcomes which are, *ex hypothesi*, mutually exclusive are combined.

Such observations are the starting point for the development of the only significant theory that has appeared to date as an alternative to the use of an expectation principle and to the use of probability as an uncertainty-variable. That theory is the work of G.L.S. Shackle (1952, 1961). On logical grounds he dismisses probability (objective or subjective) as a measure of the uncertainty or doubt about any outcome and the relevance of an expectation principle; on pseudo-empirical grounds, from alleged psychological insights, he advocates a schema for choice under uncertainty which is the antithesis of the Expected Utility Theorem.

Shackle's argument against adopting probability as a measure of uncertainty rests on two key propositions. The first is that decisions are usually non-repeatable or, as he states, non-seriable: they are unique. The second is that probability is a distributional variable: for a set of mutually exclusive outcomes, the outcomes must have a share of unity as their probability of occurrence.

The notion of probability carries the connotation that if an experiment (or action-choice) is repeated a large number of times (that is, approaching infinity), then the outcome will be $x$ with probability (relative frequency) $p$. However $p$ cannot be applied to outcome $x$ if the decision-taker can find that the choice of action which he actually makes puts him in a (say) financial position that prevents his playing the game against nature any more. This could be the likely situation in the purchase of lottery tickets, but it is probably more so in respect of the selection of an optimum portfolio, or the selection of a new machine or plant. A wrong choice could lead to the investor's wealth being dissipated.

In essence, the circumstances surrounding the selection of a particular kind of strategy will not be invariant with respect to time. For probabilities to have meaning in a choice situation, the conditions pertaining to their generation must be (strictly) unchanging; though it is usually said that this must be so within narrow bounds. This is because, *reductio ad absurdum*, if the conditions surrounding a particular event that is a constituent of a given experiment (such as, say, the tossing of a coin) were constant so that the experiment were repeated in every detail, the result should not alter (for example, the coin should still turn up heads).

More importantly, however, even if it was possible to agree that a probability density function did exist for the outcomes in a given prospect, say, for the returns expected on a new machine, that distribution would provide us with no information about the likely returns on the purchase, by an economic agent, of one extra machine. The distribution contains no assistance in predicting the returns from one machine or from the purchase of the next machine.

This point has been made forcibly in the context of gambles by A.J. Ayer (1972: 27–88, especially 27–53) in his criticism of the calculus of chances approach to probability judgements and Keynes's (1921) attempt to prove his assertion that uncertainty about a universal hypothesis is reduced (hence its probability is increased) by the addition to the available evidence of any instance in which the hypothesis is verified. It had earlier been emphasized by the distinguished American philosopher C.S. Peirce (1949), and it is a central theme in one of the authoritative writings on probability by the Cambridge statistician H. Jeffreys (1939).

Shackle, however, puts the whole matter in the most succinct and pellucid way:

> The theory of probability, in the form which has been given to it by mathematicians and actuaries, is adapted to discovering the tendencies of a *given* system under *indefinitely repeated* trials or experiments. In any set of such trials, each trial is, for the purpose of discovering such a tendency, given equal weight with all the others. No individual trial is considered to have any importance in itself for its own sake, and any tendency which may be inductively discovered, or predicted *a priori*, for the system, tells us NOTHING about any *single* individual trial which we may propose to make in future. It follows that in forming expectations, actuarial general principles and particular facts will only help us when the following conditions are satisfied:
>
> 1   We are sure that the system, whose future behaviour we wish to know, will remain a *given* system and not undergo changes during the interval of future time in question.
> 2   We are interested only in the total result of a 'large number' of trials, all of which count equally or virtually so in building up this total.
> 3   *We feel sure that we shall, in fact, have the opportunity* to carry out a sufficient number of trials, and not, for example, find that our plans depended, in fact, on the successful issue of a few early trials whose failure has deprived us of continuing (Shackle 1952: 5–6; italics in original).

Shackle's second main reason why the use of the probability calculus is incompatible with true choice under uncertainty is that probability itself is a distributional variable. In effect, the various hypothetical outcomes that characterize a prospect are assumed to be mutually exclusive, with the implication that the probabilities sum to unity. That sum is distributed across the competing outcomes. The further implication is that, if the individual decision-maker believes that another, previously unthought of, outcome is possible, at least one of the probabilities of the original outcomes in the prospect must be adjusted, in effect, reduced. Without such an effect the newly contemplated outcome could not be assigned any chance of occurrence. However, the fact that an additional outcome is conceived to be feasible might in no way affect the degree of belief that the individual attaches to the occurrence of the remaining outcomes.

Yet, the logically necessary realignment of probabilities has the corollary that he thinks the likelihood of occurrence of at least one of the existing outcomes has been reduced.

There is a paradox here. Probability, be it only subjective probability, is meant to indicate the degree of belief in the occurrence of a defined event. Yet, especially is this so with subjective probability, the apparent degree of belief in at least one specified hypothesis must alter as soon as another hypothesis is added to the inherited set: but the individual's strength of belief in the rightness of one hypothesis might not have altered. The measure he uses to encapsulate that strength must alter, however, when degree of belief is synonymous with probability. Shackle replaces probability by a new uncertainty-variable which he calls *potential-surprise*. This can be measured in degrees, but is non-distributional and non-additive. The concept can be summarized in his own words:

> The state of mind which accompanies a feeling of certainty or a high degree of belief is one of *repose*. A man who is making plans on a basis of working assumptions which he feels to be very doubtful is always, as it were, looking over his shoulder at these assumptions; on the watch for events which would compel him to abandon them ... It is only a man who feels very sure of a given outcome who can be greatly *surprised* by its non-occurrence. A degree of belief is not in itself a sensation or an emotion, but a high degree of belief is a condition of our being able to feel a high degree of surprise. The concrete mental experience which corresponds to any given degree of belief in some particular hypothesis is, I think, the degree of surprise to which this belief exposes us ... and will subject us in case the hypothesis proves false. Accordingly, we can use the degree of surprise which we judge would be caused to us by the non-occurrence of a given outcome ... as an indicator of our degree of belief in this outcome. The range of possible intensities of surprise lies between zero and that intensity which would arise from the occurrence of an event believed impossible, or held to be *certain* not to occur (Shackle 1952: 9–10; italics in original).

On the basis of the notion that degrees of potential-surprise can, and are, stipulated for uncertain outcomes or contingencies of a defined prospect, Shackle has constructed a novel and significant theory of choice under uncertainty. There are three main pillars that support his edifice. These are: the potential-surprise function; the ascendancy function; and the gambler-preference map.

The potential-surprise function replaces the probability density function in the Expected Utility paradigm: but more than that it separates out gain and loss outcomes from a course of action. The ascendancy function selects one outcome from each of the gain and loss potential-surprise functions, a kind of 'best' and 'worst' outcome, which the economic agent regards as epitomizing the promised returns from the relevant strategy. The pairs of gain, loss for each competing strategy are then compared by means of the gambler-preference map, which balances hope against fear by balancing best against worst outcome. The strategy that places the individual on the highest gambler-indifference curve is the one he selects.

Shackle's theory will be considered in more detail in Chapter 6, because the new theory of choice under uncertainty which is offered here as Perspective Theory has similarities with Shackle's theory and one version of my theory has as its foundation Shackle's strictures against the use of probability as a measure of uncertainty.

I have now formed the view that there is substantial force and merit in Shackle's arguments. In my previous book which covered Shackle's theory, *Choice, Expectation and Uncertainty* (1983), I indicated that I felt that they did have intrinsic weight; but I was also undecided as to whether Shackle's new concept of potential-surprise was an acceptable and logically sound alternative to probability. In fact, my predilection on balance was for suggesting: (a) that decision-makers would not, and could not, meaningfully rely on probability, and could be assumed to adopt a degree of uncertainty index such as potential-surprise; and (b) once formulated, however, that index for the set of outcomes defining a prospect could be transformed into a set of weights which did sum to unity. Those weights are not to be interpreted as subjective probabilities: the original thought-processes of the individual map out uncertainty about outcomes by means of potential-surprise.

The conversion to weights, pseudo-subjective probabilities if we like, permitted me to develop what I called the Shacklesque model (which others have grandly called the Fordian model) as an attempt to circumvent some of the logical inconsistencies in the schema Shackle constructed from his notion of potential-surprise as indicator of uncertainty. That model appears as Chapter 5 of *Choice, Expectation and Uncertainty*.

However, I have now also come to the view that the Shacklesque model is inappropriate: it relies on the utilization of an expectation principle, even though it does not, except in very limiting cases, rely on the Expected Utility Theorem. Even if economic agents are allowed to consider gain and loss outcomes separately from action-choices, I would wish to suggest that they will not use an averaging process by which they epitomize (in an index) the gain and the loss characteristics.

Shackle's view on this, to which it can be argued the laboratory experiments on choice under uncertainty can be seen as lending support, seem to have substance. However, the inconsistencies in this theory which I endeavoured to overcome by the Shacklesque model still remain; and there are doubts about the meaning of his uncertainty-variable, degree of potential-surprise. These matters will be discussed in more detail in Chapter 6.

Perspective Theory can be envisaged as an alternative method by which the logical inconsistencies in Shackle's theoretical framework can be circumvented. It is also a theory constructed upon a non-distributional measure of uncertainty which does not appear to suffer from the limitations of potential-surprise.

There have been attempts to shore up Expected Utility Theory or at least to preserve the use of probability and of the crucial expectation principle in the theory of choice under 'uncertainty'. It is the laboratory experiments more than anything else that have prompted those attempts: scant attention seems to have been paid to the important conceptual issues raised by Herbert Simon and, certainly since the early 1960s, not much notice has been taken of Shackle's critique of orthodoxy or of his path-breaking alternative paradigm.

The most elegant piece of research to preserve the Expected Utility approach is that of Mark Machina (1982). He has taken as his starting point the fact that the empirical evidence on the Expected Utility model casts much doubt on the independence (or substitution) axiom of the model (Axiom 4 in the Appendix to this chapter). He removes that axiom and is able to produce an optimum decision rule that should be employed by rational economic agents. This differs from that of the Expected Utility Theorem only in the sense that the probability weights are non-linear. His resulting index, whilst it can account for the laboratory experiments, is consistent with Pratt–Arrow measures of risk-aversion, and can account for the purchase of insurance, is, then, one based on probability and on a kind of expectation (averaging) principle, with gains and losses from action-choices evaluated collectively.

The two other theories that have emerged as a response to the failure of Expected Utility Theory to be verified by the facts are Prospect Theory and Regret Theory. The latter is usually taken to be originated by Kahneman and Tversky (1979): but, in fact, it has an antecedent in the works of Ward Edwards (1953, 1954a, b, c and 1955) who, in essence, produced the seminal idea. Regret Theory was advocated by Loomes and Sugden (1982).

Those theories will be summarized in Chapter 7. Yet I believe that they are lacking in many respects. Like Machina's paradigm, both of these theories rely on the use of probability distributions and Prospect Theory incorporates the spirit of the expectation principle and employs an 'average' methodology: whilst Regret Theory also merges gains and losses and incorporates an expectation principle, but without going as far as utilizing an averaging device in the fuller sense of the Expected Utility Theory model or Prospect Theory.

There have, of course, been various models proposed, based on the probability calculus, that have sought to offer 'weaker' forms of the Expected Utility construct and to recognize that aversion to losses is not perhaps adequately captured by the Expected Utility framework. One of the dominant forms has been that which, following Hicks's (1935) lead, argues that an economic agent will select that action under uncertainty which promises him the best index over the mean and variance (or standard deviation) of competing probability distributions of outcomes (*see* Markowitz 1952, 1959; and Tobin 1958). Yet others have suggested that economic agents will endeavour to avoid risk, but will take such a step by maximizing the mean value of the outcome of the given strategy subject to minimizing the probability that the outcome falls below a disaster or aspiration level. That objective was proposed by Telser (1955–56) as a follow-up to Roy's (1952) suggestion that agents would minimize the probability that the outcome *per se* of an action-choice was below a disaster level. Those Safety-First models were then amplified by Katoaka (1963) and the three models are compared in Pyle and Turnovsky (1970). They have been used quite extensively in theoretical work on the behaviour of the firm and in econometric investigation of the portfolio behaviour of financial institutions. However, they have been dominated in the literature by the Expected Utility Theory. Why? Because that theory is founded on what are regarded as a set of reasonable axioms about the behaviour of economic agents under uncertainty, axioms that obey the stochastic dominance or absolute preference criterion (*see* Axiom 5(a) of the Appendix to this chapter). The mean–variance model and the various Safety-First models noted above do not in general satisfy that criterion. (They do in very special conditions.)

The empirical evidence gives no indication that the absolute preference axiom is violated in reality. Indeed, such an axiom is the *sine qua non* of a theory of decision-making based on the probability calculus.

So, what is required is a theory of choice under uncertainty that can replace the empirically refuted Expected Utility Theory. Any new theory must at least satisfy the absolute preference axiom, but in my opinion, it must possess these further characteristics. It must recognize that individuals are averse to risk in such a way that they evaluate action-choices by weighing up their gain against their loss attributes. For most choices individuals will be imagining for themselves what are the expectational elements for particular choice-actions, they will not be confronted by fixed odd-bets, probability notions will be irrelevant and there will be no meaning that can be attached to an expectation principle. What is required is an alternative measure of belief which can be used to capture the thought-process of the individuals; and that new measure of belief, or uncertainty-variable, has to have a role in influencing action-choice other than as a weighting device in some form of averaging process. A new index of choice, in short, has to be constructed that differs from those hitherto available (except for Shackle's Theory). That index of choice must be consistent with the empirical evidence, and applicable to a variety of action-choice decisions within economics. However, in the latter regard, it must be able to locate individuals' optimal action-choice where they do have to choose fixed-odds gambles – gambles with stated probabilities. Any new theory must thus be Janus faced.

All of these requirements are very demanding when seen in sum. It is my belief that Perspective Theory, which I develop in Part II of this book, is capable of meeting those demands. Whether it will stand up against the further empirical experimentation I suggest in Chapter 8 is an open question. However, to date, for one reason or another none of the existing frameworks founded on the probability calculus can meet the requirements; indeed none can do so even if it were accepted that probability was the correct uncertainty-variable for all decisions. Shackle's theory *ex hypothesi* cannot analyse choice over probability distributions of outcomes; and his theory also contains some illogicalities with his uncertainty-variable itself being ambiguous.

# Appendix: The Axioms of Expected Utility Theory

Axioms that produce the Expected Utility Theorem have been formulated in a number of slightly different ways over the years since such a set of axioms was advanced by Von Neumann and Morgenstern (1944, 1947). Reference has already been made to the writings of Savage (1954) and Markowitz (1959): sets of axioms can be found in both of these works. The axioms that are listed here are taken from Ford (1983: Chapter 1), and are based on those of Luce and Raiffa (1957).

The following notation is employed: $C_i$ denotes choice $i$, it specifies the set of uncertain outcomes attainable from action choice $i$; $R$ denotes outcome (taken to be monetary outcome); $\pi$ denotes probability; $\succ$ means preferred to; and $\sim$ means indifferent to.

*Axiom 1: Ordering of the outcomes*
Either $R_i \succsim R_j$ or $R_j \succsim R_i$, for all $i, j = 1, \ldots, n$.

*Axiom 2: Transitivity of choices*
If $C_i \succsim C_j$ and $C_j \succsim C_k$ then $C_i \succsim C_k$.

*Axiom 3: Continuity*
With $R_1$ the most and $R_n$ the least preferred outcome, there exists some number $u_i$ where $0 \leqslant u_i \leqslant 1$, such that:
$R_i \sim [(u_i, R_1), (1 - u_i, R_n)]$; for all $i = 1, \ldots, n$.

*Axiom 4: Substitutability of outcomes and choices (Irrelevance of Independent Alternatives)*
If $R_i \sim Q_i$ then $\lambda_1 \sim \lambda_2$ where:
$\lambda_1 = [(R_1, \pi_1), (R_2, \pi_2), \ldots, (R_i, \pi_i) \ldots, (R_n, \pi_n)]$;
$\lambda_2 = [(R_1, \pi_1), (R_2, \pi_2), \ldots, (Q_i, \pi_i), \ldots, (R_n, \pi_n)]$.

*Axiom 5: Monotonity*
If (via Axiom 1) $R_i \gtrsim R_j$ and if $C_1 = [(R_i,\pi_o), (R_j,1 - \pi_o)]$ and
$C_2 = [(R_i,\pi_1), (R_j,(1 - \pi_1))]$ then:
  $C_1 \gtrsim C_2$ iff $\pi_o \geqslant \pi_1$.

*Axiom 6: The axiom of combining*
If $C_j = [(R_i,\pi_{ij}), i = 1,\ldots, n]$ for $j = 1,\ldots, m$ and if $\lambda_1 = [(C_j,a_j),$
$j = 1,\ldots, m]$ then:
  $\lambda_1 \sim \lambda_2$ where $\lambda_2 = [(R_i,\pi_i), i = 1,\ldots, n]$ and $\pi_i = \Sigma\pi_{ij}a_j$, for
$i = 1,\ldots, n$.

Axiom 5 can be cast in an alternate form which is often used in
the literature and which is a corollary of Axiom 5 as it now stands:

*Axiom 5(a): Stochastic dominance or absolute preference*
If for at least one $i = j$, $R_i \succ R_{n+i}$ and for $i = j$, $R_i \gtrsim R_{n+i}$,
for $i = 1,\ldots, n$, then $C_1 \succ C_2$ where:
  $C_1 = [(R_1,\pi_1), (R_2,\pi_2),\ldots, (R_n,\pi_n)]$;
  $C_2 = [(R_{n+1},\pi_1), (R_{n+2},\pi_2)\ldots, (R_{n+n},\pi_n)]$.

These axioms lead to the Expected Utility Theorem that an individual will be acting rationally when choosing between probability
distributions, the $(C_i)$, if he acts by maximizing the value of the
utility function, $U(.)$ where $U$ is defined by:

$$U(C) = \sum_{i=1}^{n} \pi_i u_i; \ C = [(R_i,\pi_i), i = 1,\ldots n] \tag{A1.1}$$

It will then follow that:

$$u_i = U(R_i) \tag{A1.2}$$

with the values of $u_i$ implied by Axiom 3. In effect: $0 \leqslant u_i \leqslant 1$.
Thus it can be stated that $u_n = 0$, since $R_n$ is the least preferred
outcome and $u_1 = 1$, since $R_1$ is the most preferred outcome. Then
if $\pi_1 = 1$, $C = R_1$ and:

$$U(C) = U(R_1) = u_1 \tag{A1.3}$$

we have:

$$U(C) = \sum_{i=1}^{n} \pi_i U_i(R_i) \tag{A1.4}$$

The utility function must be consistent with the preferences stated
in the axioms. Thus:

$$U(C_1) > U(C_2) \text{ iff } C_1 \succ C_2 \tag{A1.5}$$

That the conditions specified in (A1.5) hold can be proved in the
following way. Suppose that:

$$C_1 = [(R_i, \pi_i); i = 1, \ldots, n]; \text{ and } C_2 = [(R_i, q_i); i = 1, \ldots, n]$$

(A1.6)

Axioms 3 and 6 permit us to re-write $C_1$ and $C_2$ as:

$$C_1 = [(R_1, \alpha), (R_n, 1 - \alpha)]; \alpha = \sum_{i=1}^{n} \pi_i u_i$$

(A1.7)

$$C_2 = [(R_1, \beta), (R_n, 1 - \beta)]; \beta = \sum_{i=1}^{n} q_i u_i$$

(A1.8)

It then follows from Axiom 5, since $R_1 > R_n$, that:

$$C_1 > C_2 \text{ iff } \alpha > \beta$$

(A1.9)

Equation (A1.4) informs us that $U(C_1) = \alpha$ and $U(C_2) = \beta$, therefore, I conclude that (A1.5) does hold.

# 2 A Sample of Experimental Findings and Their Possible Rationalization

The preceding chapter referred to the variety of laboratory experiments that have been conducted over the past thirty or so years, and evaluated the likely empirical standing of the properties of the Expected Utility Theory, including as a concomitant an inquiry into the utility functions or preference orderings of individuals who have to choose one out of a set of competing strategies, in a situation where they cannot know in advance what the consequences of their choice will be. The only satisfactory means by which these experiments can be fully appreciated, since they are too numerous and so detailed in the bets/lotteries they have designed (in order to extract information with built-in double checks, to assess the axioms and the resulting theorem of the Expected Utility framework), is by studying the basic source materials themselves. A good, short survey of some of the major findings, however, is contained in Schoemaker (1982). For our purposes the essence of the experiments can be conveyed by surveying the most major recent findings, since, as noted in Chapter 1, they largely do no more than corroborate the earliest discoveries of Ward Edwards (1953, 1954a, b, c and 1955). Thus the research of Kahneman and Tversky (1979), noted in Chapter 1, highlights the inconsistencies that have been uncovered in respect of the orthodox model of choice under 'uncertainty'.

The experiments conducted by Kahneman and Tversky follow the earlier studies, using lottery tickets that bear the characteristics assigned to them by Edwards, Allais (1953) and, at a slightly later date, by Markowitz (1959). The Allais–Markowitz influence is, naturally, duly acknowledged by Kahneman and Tversky. The first two problems they set for the participants in their laboratory experiments were based on Allais's own examples, which led to the so-called Allais Paradox.

A group of ninety-five Stanford University students were their subjects. Most of the problems they were set were choice over gambles, lotteries or bets – however they are labelled – which had outcomes that were of a monetary magnitude. It is only gambles with such outcomes that will be of concern here. The choices to be made were between only two gambles. There were four pairs that promised only gains (or non-negative outcomes) and four pairs that promised just losses (or non-positive outcomes).

It is useful to commence by considering 'the gain' lotteries; and, for ease of comparison, the numbering of the choice problems used by Kahneman and Tversky themselves will be adopted.

The problems are paired to test the possibility that choice might be inconsistent with the axioms of the Expected Utility Theory.

*Problem 1:* Choose between

| A: | 2,500, | 0.33 | B: | 2,400, | 1.0 |
|----|--------|------|----|--------|-----|
|    | 2,400, | 0.66 |    | 0,     | 0.0 |
|    | 0,     | 0.01 |    |        |     |
| N = | 18% |    | N = | 82% |    |

*Problem 2:* Choose between

| C: | 2,500, | 0.33 | D: | 2,400, | 0.34 |
|----|--------|------|----|--------|------|
|    | 0,     | 0.67 |    | 0,     | 0.66 |
| N = | 83% |    | N = | 17% |    |

Here, each first figure is to be seen as a monetary value, measured in any currency, whilst the second figure is the probability that the lottery ticket offers for the pay out of the relevant sum. The percentage figures denote the proportions of the respondents who opted for the particular gamble. Thus, in Problem 1, the modal choice was gamble *B*; whilst in Problem 2, the modal choice was to purchase lottery *C*. Indeed, these were almost unanimous choices.

However, these two choices violate the Independence Axiom of the Expected Utility model, as Allais (1953) first demonstrated. So, the predictions of that model do not hold. If either choice of *B* or *C* satisfies the model in the one situation, the choice of the other lottery in the other situation cannot.

Thus, from Problem 1 we have if the maximization of Expected Utility guides choice:

$$U(2,400) > U(2,500)0.33 + U(2,400)0.66 \tag{2.1}$$

if we assume that $U(0) = 0$. The implication of equation (2.1) is then that:

$$U(2,400)0.34 > U(2,500)0.33 \tag{2.2}$$

However, the choice of *C* over *D* in the second set of gambles implies, if the Expected Utility Theory is true, that:

$$U(2,500)0.33 > U(2,400)0.34 \tag{2.3}$$

Why does this inconsistent pattern of choice violate the

Independence Axiom of the Von Neumann–Morgenstern framework? To answer this question, it will be noted that the axiom states (it can be, and indeed has been, stated in various forms):

If $(A,P) \succ (B,P)$                                 (2.4)
then: $[(A,P),(C,1 - P)] \succ [(B,P),(C,1 - P)]$      (2.5)

Here $(A,P)$, for example, represents a risky prospect or gamble and $\succ$ denotes 'is preferred to'. So, if the risky prospect of outcome $A$, with probability of occurrence of $P$, is preferred to outcome $B$ with probability of occurrence also of $P$, then the introduction of another, identical, risky (or, for that matter, riskless) outcome into either gamble or lottery ticket will not alter the initial choice of lottery. In effect, that choice is independent of irrelevant alternatives; which is the 'long-hand' definition of the Independence Axiom (or Substitution Axiom as Savage (1954) would label it; *see* the Appendix to Chapter 1).

It will now be observed that Problem 2 has been devised from Problem 1 by merely deducting the prospect (2,400, 0.66) from both $A$ and $B$. The prediction that risky choices will be governed by the principle of maximizing expected utility does not hold in this example, because one of the axioms underlying the principle does not hold.

Allais (1953) also demonstrated that the Substitution Axiom appears not to be applicable. That axiom is scrutinized by Kahneman and Tversky in their next pair of gambles. These can be epitomized in the following, which are only two outcome gambles; for each gamble the second outcome, namely zero and its associated probability, is omitted:

*Problem 3:* Choose between
    $A$:     (4,000, 0.80)     $B$:     (3,000, 1.0)
    $N =$    20%             $N =$    80%
*Problem 4:* Choose between
    $C$:     (4,000, 0.20)     $D$:     (3,000, 0.25)
    $N =$    65%             $N =$    35%

The choice of gamble $B$ in Problem 3 would imply, if the decision-maker's choice were motivated by the maximization of expected utility, that:

$$\frac{U(3,000)}{U(4,000)} > \frac{4}{5} \qquad\qquad (2.6)$$

However, as can be deduced, choice of $C$ over $D$ implies the inequality in (2.6) to be reversed.

Now, the Substitution Axiom asserts that:

If $A \succ B$ then $(A,P) \succ (B,P)$                    (2.7)

Here, $A$ and $B$ are prospects or gambles, of course; but they can be risky and/or riskless. In effect, they do not need to be just a single (monetary) outcome. The axiom states that if $A$ is preferred to $B$, then any risky prospect involving choice between $A$ and $B$ should always see $A$ preferred to $B$ if $A$ and $B$ are to occur with the same probability. Here, it can be seen that $C = (A, 0.25)$ and $D = (B, 0.25)$. Hence, since, in Problem 3, $B \succ A$, the order in Problem 4 should be $D \succ C$.

Problems 7 and 8 devised by Kahneman and Tversky also demonstrate forcibly the violation of the Substitution Axiom:

*Problem 7:* Choose between

| $A$: | (6,000, 0.45) | $B$: | (3,000, 0.9) |
|------|---------------|------|--------------|
| $N =$ | 14% | $N =$ | 86% |

*Problem 8:* Choose between

| $C$: | (6,000, 0.001) | $D$: | (3,000, 0.002) |
|------|----------------|------|----------------|
| $N =$ | 73% | $N =$ | 27% |

These kind of findings suggest that individuals prefer the certainty of winning, in that, where probabilities of gains are 'reasonably high', the certain gamble or that with the highest probability is selected. When the chance of winning is small (for example Problem 8), indeed, is almost indiscernible from zero, the modal preference is for the gamble offering the largest or larger gain.

The preceding gambles have all comprised non-negative monetary outcomes. Kahneman and Tversky took Problems 3, 4, 7 and 8 and reversed the outcomes to the effect that the figure previously stated as gain became a loss. In summary, the resultant gambles and the respondents' choices were:

*Problem 3a:*

| $A$: | $(-4,000, 0.8)$ | $B$: | $(-3,000, 1.0)$ |
|------|-----------------|------|-----------------|
| $N =$ | 92% | $N =$ | 8% |

*Problem 4a:*

| $C$: | $(-4,000, 0.2)$ | $D$: | $(-3,000, 0.25)$ |
|------|-----------------|------|------------------|
| $N =$ | 42% | $N =$ | 58% |

*Problem 7a:*

| $A$: | $(-3,000, 0.9)$ | $B$: | $(-6,000, 0.45)$ |
|------|-----------------|------|------------------|
| $N =$ | 8% | $N =$ | 92% |

*Problem 8a:*

| $A$: | $(-3,000, 0.002)$ | $D$: | $(-6,000, 0.001)$ |
|------|-------------------|------|-------------------|
| $N =$ | 70% | $N =$ | 30% |

Again, these choices over the pairs (3a,4a) and (7a,8a) vitiate the axioms of the Expected Utility Theorem, in the same fashion as did their equivalent gambles over gains. These findings suggest that individuals now dislike certainty, preferring large losses to small losses, provided the likelihoods of the large losses are also small. In Problem 3a, almost the whole of the ninety-five respondents preferred the loss of 4,000 with a probability of 0.8 to the sure loss of 3,000; despite the fact that the gamble chosen had a higher expected value of loss. In fact, Kahneman and Tversky (1979) concluded that there appears to be risk-seeking over negative outcomes.

As they make clear, as was noted in Chapter 1, that is a possible phenomenon observed in many previous studies. They cite Markowitz (1959), Williams (1966) and Fishburn and Kochenberger (1982); but, as seen in Chapter 1, the first, and very detailed, empirical inquiry into Expected Utility, conducted by Edwards (1953), also stressed the importance of risk-aversion for gains and risk-loving for losses. In a later summary of his findings he wrote:

> The results showed [the importance] in determining choices [of] general preferences or dislikes for risk-taking ... subjects strongly preferred low probabilities of losing large amounts of money to high probabilities of losing small amounts of money – they just didn't like to lose. It also turned out that on positive expected value bets, they were more willing to accept long shots when playing for real money, than when just imagining or playing for worthless chips (Edwards 1954, 396).

The inference that Kahneman and Tverksy drew from the preceding experimental findings was that decision-makers first of all 'edit' prospects and then choose amongst the resultants by means of Prospect Theory, as noted in Chapter 1 and outlined in Chapter 7. The editing process means, for example, that common elements in competing prospects are ignored and small differences in probabilities, across prospects for given money outcomes, which themselves are small, are also ignored. This type of editing is almost sufficient to account for the inapplicability of Expected Utility Theory to the preceding gambling choices: it removes differences between prospects, so that the elements that distinguish them in a way that is consistent with that theory have been masked.

Once the editing procedure has been accomplished, however, Kahneman and Tversky advocate the use of Prospect Theory to account for the choices of the edited-prospects. Their version of Prospect Theory differs little from the amended Expected Utility Theory advanced by Machina (1982). The only significant difference is that Machina does not assume that decision-makers edit prospects at all. Their choice is made over prospects according to a variant of the Expected Utility Theory which defines 'expected utility' to be non-linear in probabilities, so relaxing the usual expectation principle. Both Prospect Theory and Machina's model will account for the choice of lotteries presented above, which indicate a violation of the independence axiom of the Expected Utility Theory: Machina's model being, in essence, that theory without the independence axiom.

I mentioned in Chapter 1 the several alternative models of choice over probability distributions that prevail in the literature. Of those only one will explain the phenomena observed in all of the laboratory experiments; this is the 'mean, standard deviation (or variance), and skew' theory of Sir John Hicks (1967). The Hicks–Tobin–Markowitz mean–variance theory will not account for *all* of the above experimental results; nor for some of those reported by Edwards and others. Hicks's theory is not based on a utility concept. He advanced the theory for analysing portfolio selection; in the preamble to his theory he argued:

> Though the portfolio selection problem has analogies with the consumer choice problem, there is one fundamental difference. The consumer buys lemonade because he likes lemonade, but the investor does not buy ICI [shares] because he likes ICI [shares]. His investment in a particular security is solely a means to an end – the attainment of the best prospect of return over his whole portfolio. Corresponding to each distribution of placings that is available to him, within the total capital to be invested, there will be a particular prospect of return. This correspondence, though it depends upon his interpretation of the evidence that is at his disposal, has nothing to do with his *choice*. There is a choice between different prospects; some may prefer one prospect and some another. The problem is to find an index, which must refer to the total prospect, which the chooser can fairly be represented as maximising (Hicks 1967: 104; italics in original).

It is in this context that Hicks proposed an index ($I$), which depends upon the mean, standard deviation and skew of the probability distribution of any prospect. The prospect, gamble, offering the highest value of the index being the prospect selected by the decision-maker. Hicks employs the standard deviation ($S$) rather than the variance ($V$), since the former is a sum of money; for the same reason he takes skew ($Q$) to be the cube root of the third moment about the mean (even though he acknowledges that that can cause difficulties, since that moment can be negative). He labels the mean as $E$ so that the index becomes:

$$I = I(E,S,Q) \qquad (2.8)$$

The reason for including $Q$ as a risk-dimension variable besides $S$ is quite straightforward. It is easy to envisage two prospects which have the same $E$ and $S$, but one might have a negative skew, the other a positive skew. Hicks himself gives this example: prospect $A$ might have a 90 per cent chance of an outcome of four and a 10 per cent chance of an outcome of fourteen; whilst prospect B might have a 90 per cent chance of six and a 10 per cent chance of minus four. Both prospects have a mean of five and a standard deviation of three. We would not expect the individual to be indifferent between these prospects; and we would anticipate that he would select prospect A.

Intuitively, there is much to be said in favour of Hicks's index. It does suggest the individual scans the prospect under consideration, taking an overview of it in a relatively easily accomplished fashion. The mean is important, so is the spread about the mean, or its 'reliability'; but so also are possible outlying outcomes. The spread of the outcomes on the prospect can be enhanced or diminished for the individual depending upon which side of the mean the outcomes are 'stretched'. Those concepts can be thought of in everyday language; it is not necessary for every decision-maker who is choosing over 'gambles' to possess a complete knowledge of statistical theory. The Hicksian kind of overview can carry then the degree of simplicity which Heiner (1983) suggests is required of decision criteria. He argues that the complexity of decision-making in conjunction with the (likely low) degree of competence of individuals to unravel complex situations means that, inevitably, they will adopt simple rules of thumb: a position close to that of Simon (1982).

The Hicks index will explain all of the lottery ticket choices detailed earlier in this chapter, provided that skew is measured in its statistical theory sense. Thus it is the third moment about the mean divided by the standard deviation cubed. This does not produce the money value Hicks desires: but it is intuitively a better measure of skew than that used by Hicks, since it measures outliers in relation to the spread of the distribution.

What about the signs of the partial derivatives of equation (2.8)? For lotteries that offer only non-negative returns: $I_E > 0$; $I_S < 0$; and $I_Q > 0$. The sign of $I_E$ is not disputable; neither is the sign of $I_S$ for a risk-averter. If the individual is a risk-averter, then we would expect $I_Q$ to be positive: the higher are gains in relation to the mean, the more attractive the given prospect will appear to be. Should $Q$ be negative this detracts from the opportunities offered by the prospect: as a negative $Q$ becomes smaller in absolute value, of course, it is increasing; and so $I$ rises. Therefore $I_Q > 0$.

The weighting of $E$, $S$ and $Q$, naturally, could assume innumerable forms. Nevertheless, for our purposes, it will suffice if we postulate that $I(.)$ is of the simplest nature, namely it is linear in all arguments:

$$I = \alpha E + \beta S + \gamma Q; \alpha > 0, \beta < 0, \gamma > 0 \qquad (2.9)$$

If we suppose: $\alpha = 10$; $\beta = -2$; and $\gamma = 1000$, just as an illustrative example, it can be deduced that all of the modal findings for the Kahneman–Tversky 'gain lotteries' can be explained by equation (2.9). So, it could be imagined that there is an individual with the index (2.9) who is selecting one out of each pair of gambles. His choices are all consistent with that index.

Similarly, it can be posited that $I(.)$ is linear over $E$, $S$ and $Q$ for 'loss lotteries'. Now, if losses are measured as negative amounts: $\alpha > 0$; $\beta > 0$; and $\gamma > 0$, for a risk-averter. If $\alpha = 12$; $\beta = 2$; and $\gamma = 100$, all of the choices over 'loss lotteries' can be explained (remember that $Q$ is calculated using the statistical theory measure of skew). Here I have retained the assumption from the index function for gains that the individual is a risk-averter; I have then just altered the weights in $I(.)$ so that they reflect an adjustment to his degree of risk-aversion. In fact, if these lottery choices were put on the computer, it would probably be possible to deduce an $I(.)$ which accounted for choices over both types of lottery.

The mean/variance index will not permit all of the laboratory experiments to be rationalized. Neither will any variant of the A.D. Roy (1952) Safety-First model. The only probability-based competitor to Prospect Theory (including Machina's version of it) and Regret Theory capable of providing a theory that can explicate the laboratory experiments is the 'three moment theory' of Hicks.

It is an introspectively appealing theory; it goes part of the way to meet Heiner's (1983) and Simon's (1982) requirements of a realistic theory of decision-making under uncertainty. However, the Hicksian theory is one that is couched in terms of choices over probability distributions. Yet, even within that framework, even though, unlike Prospect Theory and Regret Theory, it can also be applied to a variety of choice-of-action situations (and has so been shown to be applicable, for example, to portfolio selection), it has one major deficiency, which they and the Expected Utility Theory do not possess. That defect is this: Hicks's theory will not be able to guarantee that the individual adheres to the principle of stochastic dominance. The Hicksian index of, say, the form specified in equation (2.9) could result in an individual's choosing a gain-prospect ($A$) which promises a smaller outcome in all states of nature than does another prospect ($B$); or promises the same outcome as $B$ in all states of nature except one, and in that residual state of nature it offers the promise of a lower gain than $B$ does. This criticism has been levelled more against Hicks's $(E,S)$ index but the implication of those criticisms for the $(E,S,Q)$ index has also been noted (*see* Tsiang (1972) and Borch (1974)). The simplest way of seeing this is to suppose that $I = I(E,S)$. If prospect $B$ offers a higher outcome in at least one state of nature than prospect $A$, both promis-

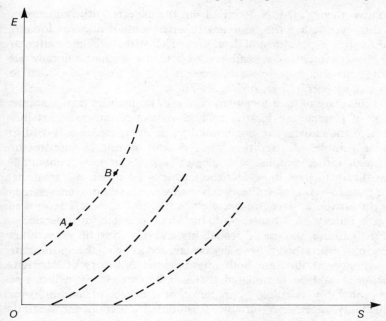

*Figure 2.1*

ing the same prospect in all other eventualities, *both* the mean and the standard deviation of *B* must exceed that of *A*. It is possible that an ordering of prospects solely in terms of the balancing of mean against standard deviation could lead, for a risk-averter, to the situation depicted in Figure 2.1. There *A* and *B* are on the same *I*-indifference curve (*B* could, of course, have been put on a lower indifference curve). However, in terms of expected utility, with actual utility dependent on money-outcomes, *B* must be preferable to *A*. In any given state of nature it promises the same or a higher outcome, hence the same or a higher value of the Von Neumann–Morgenstern utility index, each value of the index having the same probability weight across the prospects.

Even if economic agents do not follow the behavioural rule established by Expected Utility Theory, it is to be expected that stochastic dominance, which is an integral part of that theory, would be upheld in the real world. Its use requires a very simple editing process by the individual. The axiom itself has indeed been accepted by Hicks (1977).

A useful probability-based model can only lead to a two or three 'moment theory', if it is derived from the expected utility theorem. In that eventuality the 'moment theories' cannot account for any of the existing experimental data. We are left with devising an alternative theory which is compatible with both the stochastic dominance axiom and the empirical evidence on bets if we do not wish to rely on Prospect Theory or Regret Theory.

At this stage of their formulation, these two theories do not appear to be of general use for the analysis of choice under uncertainty – where the choices are not limited in number, complexity and to simple gambles. In addition, they do not appear to capture the essential, rather simple, psychological aspects of how individuals seem likely to pass in review the elements promised in prospects. The pseudo-expected value or expected value method of encapsulating the attributes over prospects embodied in Prospect Theory and Regret Theory (*see* Chapter 7) do not seem to match introspection.

Furthermore, the use of probability and of a form of 'expectation principle', even when probability is regarded as being the appropriate uncertainty-variable, are both questionable. A theory of decision-making should be formulated that can be cast either in terms of the probability calculus, or in terms of a degree of credibility or plausibility uncertainty variable. It should also account for the findings of the laboratory experiments, and be used to characterize decision-making under uncertainty in more complex and broader situations than those epitomized in the choice over lottery tickets or bets.

To accommodate those points, Perspective Theory will now be developed. That theory is based on intuition; on psychological propositions, in effect, about behaviour; but since it does explicate the experimental findings it could be argued that it has been developed *ex post facto*. Its basic framework, however, was constructed before those experiments were, indeed, studied in any depth.

# PART II
# PERSPECTIVE
# THEORY

# 3 On Perspective Theory

In this chapter I adumbrate my new theory which can account for all of the gambling phenomena presented in the preceding chapter and elsewhere. In addition, it can be applied to a whole variety of decision-making situations in economics (and perhaps also in other fields), such as the choice of portfolio of financial claims, the selection of the best strategy for real investment, the discovery of optimum levels of search, the 'to or not to insure' decision, and bargaining. The theory is based on a 'utility' approach, but its conception of 'utility' differs from that of Von Neumann–Morgenstern and, more importantly, it rejects the notion that decision-makers employ a weighted average of the utilities of outcomes from a gamble, or action-choice, in order to arrive at an overall assessment of it *per* prospect.

I hypothesize that that is so even when probabilities are objective and are taken as true by the decision-taker because the gambling odds have been stated on the lottery tickets. I also suggest that, in general, economic agents seem to use a degree of belief index, a degree of credibility index (Ayer 1972) or, reminiscent of Keynes's (1921) phrase, 'a weight of the evidence' index, for mapping out their view on the reliance they can place on what they imagine are the feasible outcomes they believe can emerge from an action-choice. They do not have objective probabilities at their disposal for the decisions they take outside of a lottery ticket framework.

My argument to support the contention that the type of expectation principle embodied in the Expected Utility Theorem is not germane to most decision-making can be stated briefly. If, as in the formulation of the theorem, it is assumed that all the outcomes contained in a prospect (of whatever kind, lottery ticket, asset portfolio) constitute an exhaustive list of mutually hypothetical outcomes, then, *ex definitione*, one of them must materialize, but only one of them can do so. Unless the experiment or action-choice can be replicated a large number of times, then there can (save fortuitously) be no purpose in 'averaging' the outcomes or their associated utilities across all outcomes. On the average, it will be the best policy to do so. After an 'infinite' number of repeated trials of the same experiment or action-choice, it will not be possible, *ex post*, to have fared better by not averaging, and hence by not having followed the expected utility maxim.

That argument has a strong affinity with the views that Professor Shackle (1952, 1961) has advocated to support his own claim that the probabilistic-based models of decision-making under uncertainty should be abandoned. His contention is that decision-taking in an economic context can be a unique decision: it may be impossible to repeat it at all, never mind on an infinite basis. The reason is simply that the choice of action might itself alter the circumstances surrounding that choice. As an example, the choice to be made might relate to the best portfolio of financial assets that should be held. Whatever choice is made will affect future wealth and it could emerge as a choice that produced losses and so reduced the individual's stock of wealth. That fact could make it impossible for the choice to be repeated, since one of the control variables on portfolio selection, obviously, is the level of wealth available for the purchase of investments. In a more vivid, Shacklesque fashion it can be said that the choice of portfolio could result in the individual's being out of the game.

Shackle also has other objections to the probabilistic approach to the modelling of choice under uncertainty. One of these is a corollary of the preceding point in that he believes that objective probabilities can only be used for repeatable experiments, since they derive their own meaning and status to knowledge, as relative frequencies, from repeatable experiments. Another objective is a corollary of this: since relative frequencies are knowledge over a repeatable, serial, experiment, it follows that if the experiment is a serial one, as required by the use of objective probability, then the result of the experiment is known 'in the large'. There is no uncertainty. Only risk is present; and then only so for an individual, unique, experiment – not for an experiment that is repeatable or explicitly pooled (hence implicitly repeatable, like insurance). His final objection to the application of probability to the analysis of decision-making under uncertainty concerns the implications of the probability calculus itself. *Ex definitione*, the probabilities of mutually exclusive outcomes, or events, must sum to unity; and there is a scale for probability bounded at zero and one. There are two implications of these constraints. The first is that if the individual revises his view as to the outcomes that are feasible for a particular choice of action, the probability of occurrence of at least one existing outcome must be revised: and by an artefact. The second consequence is that only one outcome can be accorded the maximum degree of belief, of unity.

Shackle's own index of belief, or degree of dis-belief, we should say, does not suffer from those drawbacks. Also, his theory of choice under uncertainty does not follow the 'averaging' process of the

Von Neumann–Morgenstern school, which he found objectionable.
I shall provide an exposition of Shackle's schema in Chapter 6 where
it is compared with my own theory.

For the moment it is advisable to pause at these strictures on
the validity of the probabilistic approach, and turn to my own theory.
In brief, my suggested theory, which I shall label Perspective Theory,
can be set forth as follows. To begin with we must summarize the
variant of Perspective Theory where it is assumed that decision-
makers are faced by fixed odd gambles or lotteries. That is to say,
the outcomes in the gambling prospects are assigned probabilities
which are objective or are taken to be so.

There are four basic postulates:

(i)    If prospects embrace both gains and losses, then the gain
and loss elements will be segregated.

(ii)    The gain and loss outcomes for any prospect are encapsulated
separately, in a number or, if preferred, an index, to be
called an *ascendancy index,* because of its connotation (and
despite its similarity to one of the key elements in Professor
Shackle's theory). That index is, in effect, the maximum
(real) number that the individual assigns to the *ascendancy
function*; this measures the attractiveness to him of the gain
aspects of any prospect, and the maximum unattractiveness
of its loss aspects.

     The two ascendancy functions have as their arguments
monetary outcome and an associated probability of occurrence (to be defined shortly). The two versions of the
function need not be identical. Up to a point there are,
*prima facie*, reasons for supposing that they are, since both
are concerned, as it were, with maximum values of utility
or dis-utility. However, because one aspect of risk-aversion
is implied in the proposition that gains and losses are viewed
separately, and in the light of the empirical and intuitive
evidence (*see* Chapters 1 and 2) regarding attitudes to losses,
it is possible that the specific form of the ascendancy function
for losses would differ from that for gains. That is a question
of substance and detail which I shall pursue shortly. At
this juncture, one minor particular must be noted before
continuing my outline of the pillars of Perspective Theory.
That is that the ascendancy function for gains is labelled
as phi, $\phi(.)$, and that for losses as psi, $\psi(.)$, to allow for
potential dis-similarity between the functions.

(iii)    The choice of action, gamble, or whatever, that is to be
effected, is accomplished by an action choice-index which
I call the *Perspective Index* (*PI*). That index is a balancing

of the 'best' on the gain side and the 'worst' on the loss side that any prospect appears to offer to the individual decision-taker. This too can be envisaged in line with familiar, orthodox, choice theory under certainty, by thinking of it as a 'utility' indicator which is the value of the function $PI = P(\phi^\star, \psi^\star)$; where the asterisks on $\phi$ and $\psi$ are used to remind us that the action-choice index is based on a weighing up of the highest, 'best', values of $\phi(.)$ and of $\psi(.)$. It is a form of net utility index.

(iv)   Whatever the prospects that offer themselves to the individual, so that they might consist of all gains or of all losses, I hypothesize that he evaluates a $PI$ for each prospect that depends upon a highest and a lowest value of whichever ascendancy function is appropriate. So, if there is a risky prospect which promises only gain outcomes, the action-choice index is transformed into: $PI$ is the maximum of $P(\phi^\star, \phi_{min})$. Hence, $\phi_{min}$ replaces $\psi^\star$.

The alternative variant of this schema differs from the above in postulating that instead of prospects consisting of a pair of values (monetary outcome, probability), they are to be seen in most contexts as pairs of monetary outcome, subjective degree of belief or credibility. There will be situations in which the use of probabilities is valid, but in those situations Perspective Theory stipulates that they are not used as weights in an averaging process across a prospect's outcomes in order to yield an indicator of its psychic value. *Ergo*, for those who wish to persist in retaining the view that everyday language does suggest that subjective probability is used ('this does not have much chance of success' or 'I would say the odds are two to one against a fall in interest rates' . . .), Perspective Theory based on objective probability covers that case, *ex hypothesi*.

I shall come to the index of credibility later. For now, the main pillars of Perspective Theory will be amplified as catalogued in (i) to (iv). Let me take them *seriatim*.

Any theory is founded on a set of axioms and the theorems or predictions that follow as deductions from the axioms. There is nothing in meta-theory that permits us to state that one set of axioms or postulates is better than any other because they are somehow intrinsically right; despite the claims sometimes made to the contrary, as mentioned in Chapter 1.

It seems clear, though, that risk-aversion plays an important role in determining an individual's behaviour under uncertainty, and that it will lead to losses playing a significant part in the overall assessment of gambles, investments or whatever the concern of action-choice happens to be. In respect of risky prospects or ventures, the possibility of loss, largely related to the current wealth position, especially for the 'ordinary' consumer and business man, will figure prominently in his calculations as he does take a *perspective* on the prospects that are available to him.

Apart from the introspective feeling that there is an overriding desire of Safety-First, we have the large body of cumulative evidence from the laboratory experiments of the past thirty years. It offers overwhelming evidence that losses are accorded a special role in the minds of decision-makers; and that frequently their attitude to the possibility of loss differs from that shown towards gains – precisely because of a Safety-First element in their behaviour.

The possible need to recognize the separate impact of losses on decision-makers' impressions of prospects, however, was well-recognized before the laboratory experiments commenced. The whole of Professor Shackle's (1949, 1961) own novel and imaginative approach to the modelling of action-choice under uncertainty is predicated on that need. Andrew Roy's 'Safety-First model of asset choice' (1952) is of the spirit. The more recent attempts to amplify the mean–variance model by introducing the notion that individual decision-takers constrain their choice of action by the self-imposed need to make a minimum return or gain on, for example, any investment portfolio, come within that category.[1]

It would be fair to postulate that, in all possible ways, evidence exists in support of the notion that, where present in uncertain prospects, losses should be evaluated on their own merits, and not be subsumed, averaged, with gains. What about circumstances, however, where either gains or losses, but not both, are promised? Our hypothesis is that individual decision-makers will still consider a 'best' and a 'worst' index from, say, a gamble that offers solely the prospect of gains.

It might be hypothesized that, in terms of human psychology, this is indeed the more likely to be so, the greater is the number of alternative outcomes that any one prospect (gamble, lottery ticket, financial asset portfolio, insurance policy . . .) appears to offer to the individual. However, even for those prospects that offer as few as two possible outcomes, I would submit that the human psyche is such that for those averse to risk, in whatever degree, the prospect is scanned and the most appealing and unappealing aspects are highlighted. Since only one outcome can actually materialize, no risk-averse individual will select just one outcome (with assigned degree of probability or belief) as encapsulating, as setting in perspective, any prospect. The best that it can promise, bearing in mind its chances of occurring, will be balanced against the worst that it could produce. It would be foolhardy to concentrate on just the best, except in a world where that 'best' was represented by a certain outcome; I do not say that it would be irrational to place, as it were, one's eggs in one basket. It follows, by implication, however, from our behavioural postulates that it would be irrational for an individual to do so if he felt that his behaviour could be described by our postulates or axioms.

Two factors of importance must be stressed. The first, which is the more straightforward and can be disposed of expeditiously, is this. Should our objective be one of solely describing a framework of decision-making under uncertainty, which can explain away the finding of the multifarious laboratory experiments, it would be sufficient to postulate that the individual's choice of lottery ticket will be the one that maximizes the value of $\phi$ or, as apposite, minimizes the value of $\psi$. A preference-ordering over monetary outcome and associated probability (or degree of belief) which is maximized, for gains, can readily be constructed which satisfies all of the choices epitomized in the problems listed in Chapter 2 above.

The second factor that should be emphasized is that the individual takes an overview, a perspective, of all of the outcomes promised by a gamble. He weighs up the outcomes across the feasible range, bearing in mind their likelihood of occurrence (or degree of credibility). Very high gains can be offset, discounted, in his mind if they have low degrees of credibility. However, if their degree of credibility is sufficiently encouraging, those high gains will be discounted very little. They will be the focus of the decision-taker's attentions, but, as he holds the set of outcomes in his purview, his imagination is caught by the worst outcome (given its degree of credibility) that might just ensue from the selection by him of this particular gamble. The two pillars, as it were, leap out at him; they give a focus to, an encapsulation of, the relevant prospect.

I have suggested that where only gains or losses are imagined, it is feasible that, in specified contexts, the decision-maker might set a lower limit, an aspiration level, that a chosen strategy must be capable of providing. In my framework, this would be depicted, for gains, by the lowest $\phi$ values that the decision-maker would require before he contemplates making a given choice of strategy. Only those strategies would be in the efficient set which promised a minimum $\phi$-value at least equal to the $\phi$-aspiration level. Thereafter, the selected course of action would be the alternative that gave hope of the highest $\phi$-value.

This Simonesque variant for Perspective Theory does not differ from the latter in spirit and barely at all in the letter. I shall refer to it in Chapter 5. I have suggested that it is too ambitious to hope that we can devise a model of decision-making under uncertainty that has universal validity. However, I also do not wish to develop what I propose into a series of *ad hoc* formulations, a kind of patchwork quilt to suit all occasions, even if there is an underlying thread that links all elements of each quilt, as it were.

So, I shall retain my hypothesis that 'best–worst' Perspective Theory is the paradigm that can be used, as a unified structure, to describe choice under uncertainty. The process of decision-making will follow the lines established above, no matter whether the uncertainty-variable is distributional or non-distributional.

Some further observations on $\phi(.)$ and hence upon $\psi(.)$ are now appropriate. The $\phi$ function is defined over gains and the uncertainty-variable. If the latter is probability $(\pi)$, then I would argue that it is to be envisaged as the probability that the associated monetary gain at the least will be attained. In effect, it is one minus the value of the cumulative distribution function for gains at the prescribed value of gain. $\phi(.)$ will be increasing, separately, in monetary gain and probability. It may be assumed that $\phi(.)$ is continuous for the sake of formal analysis. Accordingly, there will exist a trade-off between monetary outcome and probability along any $\phi$ indifference curve. It is also taken to be an axiom that $\phi$ indifference curves are convex in (gain, probability) space.

Now, these axioms mean that stochastic dominance is satisfied by $\phi(.)$. Why? Because if over gains, $1 - F(x) > 1 - F(y)$, for all $x = y$ where $x$ and $y$ are monetary gains in 'gamble' $X$ and $Y$, $\phi_x > \phi_y$. Thus, the positive ascendancy, the 'utility', of gamble $X$ exceeds that of gamble $Y$; and, *ceteris paribus* by $P(.)$, $X$ would be preferred to $Y$. Or, in the weak form of stochastic dominance, if for at least one $x = y$, $1 - F(x) > 1 - F(y)$, and for all other $x = y$, $1 - F(x) = 1 - F(y)$, it would follow that $\phi_x > \phi_y$. The $\psi$ function is defined over losses (taken as their absolute values) and the relevant uncertainty-variable. If the latter is taken to be probability, it will be seen as the probability that at least the associated level of loss will occur. So, again, for $\psi(.)$ *per se* stochastic dominance holds.

Therefore, since $P = P(\phi\cdot, \psi\cdot)$ is increasing in $\phi$ and decreasing in $\psi$ with $\phi\cdot$, and $\psi\cdot$ being the maximum values of positive and negative ascendancy, utility and dis-utility, associated with any gamble, it must follow that $P(.)$ implies that stochastic dominance obtains. Thus, if one gamble $(X)$ dominates another $(Y)$ stochastically we have $\phi_x > \phi_y$ and $\psi_x < \psi_y$, therefore, $P_x > P_y$.

It will be noted that $P(.)$ defines the choice over gambles. $\phi(.)$ and $\psi(.)$ are not to be thought of in that way; so that a gain expectational element (monetary outcome $(x)$, probability $(\pi)$) is assigned a number $\phi$. It is *not* $[(x, \pi), (o, 1 - \pi)]$ that is assigned a $\phi$-value, as would have to be the case if $\phi(.)$ had been axiomized over gambles, other than over expectational-elements, as here. If $\phi(.)$ had been so defined, $\psi(.)$ could not exist; neither could $P(.)$. Gains and losses would have been considered together in the index assigned to any gamble: and so the real numbers attached to the expectational elements within a gamble, viewed *per* gamble, would have been Von Neumann–Morgenstern utility units. Consequently, the consistent ranking of gambles by rational economic agents would have had to assume the form established in the Expected Utility Theorem.

The above comments cover the situations where the uncertainty-variable happens to be a measure of probability. For completeness, it is necessary to offer some remarks for instances (which I regard as more frequent and germane, where the uncertainty-variable is the kind of degree of belief or credibility index ($\theta$) I shall discuss shortly. Take $\phi(.)$, as an example. It will depend positively upon gain and $\theta$: the latter will represent the degree of belief in the respective monetary gains. By construction, there is no meaning attached to the addition of degrees of belief; and hence the notion of the degree of belief in an outcome at least as great as some magnitude cannot exist.

## The Degree or Index of Credibility or Belief

Turning to the structure of a degree of credibility uncertainty-variable which can act as an alternative to objective or subjective probability, it is possible that an index of credibility or degree of belief might be axiomatized in the following:

i　The imagined rightness of any hypothesis concerning the outcome of any course of action is encapsulated in the degree of credibility or belief in the occurrence of that hypothesis;

ii　The degree of credibility or belief can be zero; in which case the individual regards the relevant hypothetical outcome as impossible;

iii　The scale of degree of belief is bounded above by some number $\bar{\theta}$, which denotes the individual's view that the hypothesis to which it is attached will occur with certainty;

iv　All rival hypotheses regarding the outcome of some specified experiment or action-choice can carry the same degree of credibility, except the degree of $\bar{\theta}$;

v　The degree of belief that is attached to any hypothesis, $H$, must be the highest degree that is associated with what the individual regards as the set of hypotheses which themselves seem to the individual to induce $H$.

There are four corollaries to these axioms:

1 The range of degree of belief is o to $\bar{\theta}$; with $\bar{\theta}$ possibly differing between individuals;

2 If any one of a set of potentially competing hypotheses is assigned the value $\bar{\theta}$, all other hypotheses must be assigned a zero value of $\theta$.

3 Out of a set of rival hypotheses at least one hypothesis must carry a degree of belief greater than zero. Thus, suppose that there are only three possible hypotheses, $H_1$, $H_2$ and $H_3$. If all are assigned a degree of belief of zero, there exists a logical contradiction. The individual's information set leads him to the conclusion that: either $H_1$ or $H_2$ or $H_3$ must be correct. To attach a zero degree of belief to $H_1$, $H_2$ and $H_3$ would be logically inconsistent.

4 A corollary of 3 arises for the special case of two hypotheses $H_1$ and $H_2$. If either $H_1$ or $H_2$ is assigned a degree of belief of zero, the other must be assigned a degree of belief of $\bar{\theta}$.

What about the scale for $\theta$? There is no reason why this should not be assumed to be from zero to unity. A $\bar{\theta}$ of unity would not imply that 'degree of belief' was equivalent to a subjective probability and hence a distributional variable. However, a degree of belief is a weight of the evidence, a chance-of-occurrence, concept; and since individuals' strengths of feeling in the correctness of hypothetical outcomes are usually expressed in terms of probabilities, it is likely to be more empirically sound to conceive of degree of belief as measured in a similar fashion. In that case, the supposition would be that $\bar{\theta}$ does not differ between individuals.

Such a postulate would not render $\theta$ a distributional variable. Only in the special case of a prospect with an hypothesis to which was attached a value of $\bar{\theta}$ could it follow that the introduction of an alternative, competing, outcome into an existing prospect might of necessity alter any existing $\theta$. Thus assume that, originally, the individual envisaged two hypothetical outcomes $H_1$ and $H_2$, with $\theta_1 = \bar{\theta}$ and $\theta_2 = 0$ (where subscripts denote the relevant hypotheses). If he now believes that a third hypothesis is possible, $H_3$, to which he does accord a positive $\theta$, it must follow that $\theta_1$ is reduced below $\bar{\theta}$. However, it is possible, for example, that (the new) $\theta_1 = \theta_3 < \bar{\theta}$. The same, but less than certain, belief can be assigned to two outcomes; and $\theta_1 + \theta_3 \gtreqless \bar{\theta}$.

We must not be led into constructing arguments of the following genre. Should the individual postulate that $H_1$, $H_2$, ..., $H_n$ define a prospect, which consists of an exhaustive list of mutually exclusive hypotheses, the degree of belief attached to the set *per se* must be $\bar{\theta} = 1$. Accordingly, the sum of the $\theta$s must be unity. Only if the

$\theta$ are defined as subjective or objective probabilities, hence as relative frequencies with the base of these relative frequencies being the set $H$ itself, can we, must we, find, and then it is so by construction, that the $\theta$s sum to unity.

It will always be easy to fall into that kind of view if $\bar{\theta}$ is set at unity. However, there is no advantage, other than eliminating the likelihood of such arguments, from permitting $\theta$ to possess any other upper bound, such as ten or one hundred, since this would only lead to an index that is a simple scalar of that defined over the unit interval: that is, except for the possibility that the maximum value of $\theta$ could differ between individuals.

Suppose that the hypotheses that the individual was formulating were concerned with political, rather than economic, events, to take a simple and immediate example, such as the result of the next general election in the UK. There will be several parties that will contest the election. However, the three main ones will be: Conservative, Labour, and SDP–Liberal Alliance. A zero degree of belief would certainly be attached to the chances of the fringe parties, such as the Ecology (or Green) Party, of obtaining a majority of seats in the House of Commons. On current opinion polls (at the time of writing: March 1986) and given the political ramifications of the saga over the Westland Helicopter Company (January–February 1986), a lower degree of belief would be attached to a Conservative victory than to a victory for either of the other two parties. A high, and equal, degree of belief would be attached to either of the other two parties winning the election: there is no reason to favour the one over the other. So, $\theta$ might be set at these values: 0.4 for the Conservative Party; 0.8 for both the Labour Party and the SDP–Liberal Alliance.

The seemingly paradoxical nature of that statement, and of the preceding arguments, can be dispelled by thinking of degree of belief as degree of credibility. I have used belief and credibility interchangeably. They are synonymous, but there is no doubt that the essence of the uncertainty of any hypothesis is best captured by the use of credibility rather than belief. In its everyday interpretation, the credibility attached to, the seeming possibility of, two hypothetical outcomes can be the same. Essentially, of course, the two words are the same: but it is just that the one seems better to convey the feelings about uncertainty than the other!

## The Application of Perspective Theory in Outline

A 'descriptive' summary of Perspective Theory was provided in the early sections of this chapter. I will now indicate how it is used,

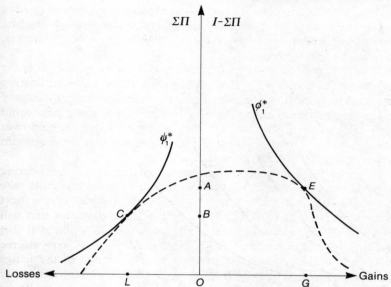

*Figure 3.1*

adopting a more formal approach. Specific applications will be presented in full in Chapters 4 and 5.

Suppose an individual decision-maker, who might be a consumer, a business man, or whatever, has to select a strategy out of two alternatives, $S_1$ and $S_2$. He first of all maps out the expectational elements, comprising, let it be assumed, both 'gains' and 'losses' for each strategy. Let these be described by a discrete subjective probability distribution; which is represented in Figure 3.1 by the dotted line. There the sum of the probabilities ($\pi_i$) should sum to unity, but the diagram has not been drawn to scale, for illustrative purposes. $\Sigma\Pi$ denotes the sum of probabilities up to a given loss; $1 - \Sigma\Pi$ is the probability of obtaining a gain in excess of the given value (strictly, of obtaining at least that value).

$\phi_1^*$ is the highest value of utility or desirability $\phi$ that can be attained given the constraint on $\phi(.)$ imposed by the discrete probability distribution over gains: $OG$ and $OA$ represent the expectational element at which $\phi(.)$ is maximized. Likewise, $\psi_1^*$ is the worst level of dis-utility that the individual believes the strategy $S_1$ offers. (Note here that I have let $\psi(.) \neq \phi(.)$; so that $\psi$ can be more responsive to outcomes than $\phi$ if we so wish, in accordance with the empirical evidence of Chapter 2.)

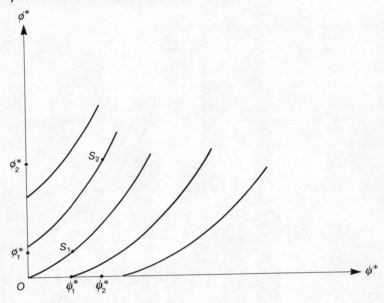

*Figure 3.2*

The same exercise is completed for $S_2$ and values, say, of $\phi_2^\star$ and $\psi_2^\star$ are obtained. These two strategies can now be evaluated by means of the perspective function, since with $\phi_1^\star < \phi_2^\star$ and $\psi_1^\star < \psi_2^\star$ one strategy does not dominate the other stochastically. The comparison, of course, depends upon the loss-averse ('risk'-averse) nature of the individual, since this will condition the weight he attaches to any value of $\psi^\star$. Assume that $P(.)$ is such as to generate the ordering described by the $P$-indifference curves illustrated in Figure 3.2.

As illustrated, Strategy 2 will be chosen. Strategy 1 leads the individual to expect that he will do no better than a do-nothing solution.

Figure 3.2 can be extended to continuous distributions and numerous alternative strategies. Additionally, when $\theta$ replaces $\pi$, the analytical procedure is in essence identical with that summarized above.

In Chapters 4 and 5 I shall provide detailed analysis of Perspective Theory when applied in a variety of decision-making contexts in economics. In Chapter 6 I offer some comparisons between Perspective Theory and Shackle's Theory in modelling specific choices of action.

# Notes

1 Sir John Hicks (1977: Essay VIII) has now come to the view that such rates
of return (what he, like Andrew Roy (1952), labels disaster rates of return) should
play a prominent role in the construction of models of asset-choice. Nevertheless
it is interesting to observe that his formulation involves an amendation of the
Expected Utility Theory, which, for the most part, he finds he cannot accept
(*see* Hicks 1967: Chapter VI). His suggestion is that each imagined return on
each asset is scaled down by the (per unit) disaster rate of return; the rate of
return below which the investor, be he an individual or an investment fund
manager, would find himself faced by financial ruin. The investor is supposed
to select that portfolio which will maximize the expected value of the 'utility'
to be received from 'above disaster level' of returns. Such an approach, being
a mere transformation of asset returns, does not provide an approach that can
offer anything over and above that provided by the orthodox representation of
Expected Utility. Thus, it cannot be employed as a means of rescuing the Expected
Utility Theorem from its failure to account for the laboratory experiments referred
to in Chapter 2.

# Appendix: An n-Dimensional Version of Perspective Theory

Sir Charles Carter has kindly endorsed the ideas promulgated here on Perspective Theory, in both of its versions. However, he has suggested that the theory I have outlined in Chapter 3 is a special case of a more general theory. His argument is that either version of Perspective Theory can be taken as applying to a state of the world, or scenario, as he prefers to call it. What is required, he continues, is a theory that extends to $n$ scenarios.

The exposition of Perspective Theory contained in Chapter 3 can be interpreted as applying to $n$ scenarios with the supposition being that only one outcome for each action-choice is expected to occur in each scenario. That is the usual hypothesis in the application of the Expected Utility Theory; although the latter can readily handle the case where there is a probability density function for the states of nature or scenarios (this can be deduced, if the reader so wishes, from Axiom 6 of the Expected Utility Theory axioms stated in the Appendix to Chapter 1). In such a situation the individual would still be able to reduce the promised outcomes from any action-choice or strategy to a probability density function and apply the Expected Utility Theorem in the familiar way.

Let us assume that there do happen to be, in the individual decision-maker's opinion, $n$ states of the world. How would Perspective Theory incorporate that fact? The answer that Carter believes Perspective Theory should give to this is as follows (which he has agreed is in accord with the comments he has made to me). To each scenario there will be a gain and a loss ascendancy function, or utility/dis-utility function, as described and formulated in Chapter 3. Therefore, many outcomes are feasible for any scenario. For each and every scenario there will be a value of $P(.)$. Accordingly, each strategy or action-choice will be represented by some $Z(.)$, where:

$$Z = Z(P_1, P_2, \ldots, P_n) \tag{A3.1}$$

So, a comparison of $Z_i$ has to be effected; and that comparison will select the action-choice that the individual adopts, rather than comparisons of $P_i$ for the competing action-choices, as was the case in

Chapter 3. How will the $Z_i$ be compared? We must posit that $Z(.)$ obeys stochastic dominance. So, if for at least one state of nature $P_A > P_B$ and for all other states of nature $P_A = P_B$, then strategy $A$ will be chosen in preference to strategy $B$: $Z_A > Z_B$.

However, for the case of several states of nature it cannot be expected that the individual would have an ordering over all of the $P_i$. Unless the states of nature were a mere handful, say, up to three, he will use, I would suggest, an ordering over $Z(.)$ which consists of the *highest* and the *lowest* values of $P_i$ for any action-choice.

Such a procedure, whilst following the spirit of the construction of the $P$-function in Chapter 3, is very much in line with the spirit of Perspective Theory *per se*, which is a theory that imagines the individual to be simplifying the complex set of outcomes and choices available to him. The $Z$-function then it may be supposed is:

$$Z_i = Z_i(P_{i\,\text{max}}, P_{i\,\text{min}}) \tag{A3.2}$$

The partial derivatives of $Z_i(.)$ would both be positive (unlike the two derivatives of $P(.)$).

Now, Carter has indicated that in his opinion decision-making under uncertainty by individuals exhibits two key features: the first is that they attempt to simplify the range of expectational elements by concentrating on a few highly believeable outcomes, and so discarding those that have a low degree of belief; the second is that the individual psyche can only assimilate a very limited number of scenarios, so that the feasible set of scenarios is also reduced to very few in number (*see* his own theory in Carter 1953). Thereafter, Carter seems to accept that something like a perspective index is evaluated for each strategy for each state of the world. However for each strategy there will be a $Z(.)$ consisting of more than one element, but at the most having only a small number.

He accepts that choice will be effected by a $Z(.)$ which satisfies the absolute preference or stochastic dominance axiom, but where there are more than two $P$ values for any $Z(.)$ it is not clear how he imagines the final act of choice to be accomplished. I have gained the impression from his observations that, since at the most $Z(.)$ will contain, say, four or five values of $P$, the individual will utilize all values of $P$ carrying out a comparison of action-choices. He lays more stress on a comparison of $Z_i$ *per se* than on the valuation that should be placed on each $Z_i$. Obviously, once a weighting system has been posited for the $P_i$ in each $Z(.)$, there exists a means of placing a number on any $Z_i$ and, hence, of comparing the various $Z_i$ for the competing action-choices. Carter, however, seems to be arguing for a kind of ordinal comparison of the $Z(.)$.

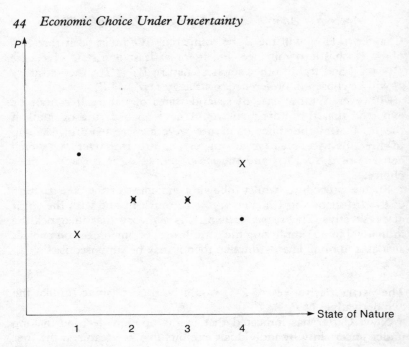

*Figure A3.1*

So, suppose that the individual has two strategies ($A$ and $B$) over which he is choosing (these might be thought of as two pieces of machinery) and he assumes that four states of the world are all that are worth considering. Let the $P$-values for the strategies in the four states of the world be as portrayed in Figure A3.1.

The crosses denote $P$-values for strategy $A$, the dots for strategy $B$. Note that in states of nature 2 and 3, $P_A = P_B$. In state of nature 1, $P_B > P_A$, whilst in the state of nature 4 the opposite is true. In an instance such as this Carter would suggest that *hedging* is likely to occur; the individual chooses to invest in both machines because the one does not offer a demonstrably clear advantage over the other.

A weighting procedure for evaluating a $Z(.)$, which merely gave equal weights to the $P$s, would rank $B$ above $A$. A weighting procedure over the $P$-values, which permitted a value of $Z$ to be calculated following the lines specified in equation (A3.2), would also produce that ranking.

It would seem appropriate to maintain the notion that, where stochastic dominance or near stochastic dominance does not hold over the sets of $P$-values for the competing strategies, that equation

(A3.2) will be employed as the ranking device in the case of several states of nature; especially so if the number of strategies is not very small.

As stated, the kind of procedure epitomized in equation (A3.2) is in the spirit of that embodied in Perspective Theory as outlined in Chapter 3. Its essential characteristic is that 'averaging' does not occur: the individual knows that only one $P$-value for any strategy can occur, but he has to cover himself for the fact that he does not know which one that will be. The range of possibilities across the state of the world is what he will consider.

It might be argued, as a corollary to that observation, that each $P$-value will be assigned a probability of occurrence or degree of belief by the individual, which applies to the state of the world which it is supposed will produce that $P$-value. Therefore, why does the individual not have a $Z(.)$ that contains a set of pairs of $(P, \text{probability})$? Such a process would be too complex; it runs counter to the simplification process and to the fact that as part of that process only few states of nature are regarded as feasible: they are likely to have probabilities or degrees of belief, therefore, within a small band.

Having said all this it must be reiterated that there is an alternative means by which several states of nature can be accommodated; that is, the means adopted in Chapter 3, where for each (of many) states of nature only one outcome was thought to be feasible.

A completely different method of approach can also be adopted. This is the one often used in the probability-based literature. It supposes that for any strategy, such as the investment of wealth in government bonds, the individual maps out the feasible range of returns. These will be bounded, having a small range given recent experience and future expectations of changed conditions in financial markets. Then to each return the investor assigns a degree of probability of occurrence or degree of belief. For portfolio investment this is more likely to be the method that is followed; and the range of outcomes is reduced and simplified. In that way a probability density function or degree of belief function materializes. That also is an interpretation that can be accorded to the expectational elements in Perspective Theory in Chapter 3: so that there is no intrinsic need to consider a states of the world approach and to dwell necessarily on the number of those states. Indeed, even if I were to do so for the version of Perspective Theory based on the degree of belief index, any outcome would be assigned only one degree of belief by Axiom v upon which the index is founded.

# 4 Perspective Theory and Portfolio Selection

One of the major contexts, ouside that of the gambling or lottery ticket environment, in which any successful theory of decision-making under uncertainty must be applicable is that of portfolio choice. The latter, in its more general form, will encompass the selection of both assets and liabilities. Naturally, in a developed financial market, the choice of liabilities can be an important influence on the performance of the whole portfolio of financial claims.

The conventional literature has tended to focus its attention on the choice by individual investors, be they individuals, business firms, financial institutions (or even governments), of the best set of *assets* to hold at any time. For the most part, but by no means exclusively, that choice has usually been analysed in a pseudo-static, one-period-at-a-time decision-process. Dynamics, however, has not gone unanalysed.

In what follows, to keep the analysis as straightforward as possible, I shall assume that investors can indeed only choose *assets*. It is a simple step to extend the analysis to cover the existence of liabilities.

Also, I shall confine my analysis to 'static' models since my primary objective is to demonstrate the ability of Perspective Theory to handle questions of portfolio selection and management. The implications involved in dynamic structures only serve to make the analysis more complex without adding much of substance.

The *probability version* of Perspective Theory can be thought of as being couched in terms of either objective or subjective probabilities. In most treatments of asset-choice, a number of simplifying assumptions are made to make the analysis manageable, even in the static framework. The most important of these is that individual investors participate in a perfect capital market, which possesses the central corollary that the gains or losses, positive or negative yields, that an individual might expect from investment in any financial claim, can be taken by him to be independent of his own purchases of that claim. He cannot, in short, turn the prices of financial claims against himself or to his own advantage.

It is clear that to make such a supposition does simplify the analysis considerably. Without invoking it the investor would have to choose his portfolio of assets by taking into account the simultaneity between that selection and the gains/losses he might expect as a consequence; those gains/losses themselves helping to determine his optimum port-folio. I shall, therefore, retain the assumption of perfect competition in money and financial markets.

The two other assumptions that are almost invariably used are that: there are no transactions costs involved in buying and selling assets; and there is no expectation of inflation on behalf of the individual investors. The first assumption, whilst obviously unrealis-tic, is innocuous if transactions costs are fixed (that is, do not vary with the quantity or value of the assets traded) and are identical for all transactions. In that case, transactions costs can be filtered out of the analysis; they have no independent role to play in affecting the (net) gains/losses on financial investments. Since inflation must, naturally, influence all real returns on assets to the same extent, even if investors do believe that there will be inflation, it can be ignored in the evaluation of the optimum portfolio, provided the investor is operating within a 'static' framework: he reviews his port-folio at the end of each period, the latter being any unit of time; the supposition being that he only looks to hold the chosen portfolio for a period. Accordingly, I too shall make these two assumptions. In contrast to the rescinding of the perfectly competitive assumption, making allowance for transactions costs and for expected inflation does not increase unduly the complexity of the analysis.

I shall assume that the individual investor has drawn up a series of probability distributions on the gains/losses that are promised by each of a set of financial claims. Again, the gains/losses can be thought of as representing positive/negative yields; it is those yields, of course, that determine if there are gains/losses, or increases to invested wealth, from a particular portfolio allocation.

As with Expected Utility Theory, the investor has to 'scale up' the probability distribution of 'returns' on the individual assets to permit him to compare portfolios that exhaust his wealth. For each possible portfolio, be it the holding of all of his wealth in one asset, or the placing of wealth across the whole range of alternative assets, he has to calculate the relevant porfolio probability distribution of returns.

In the Expected Utility approach such a task, effectively, does not need to be undertaken. There is a direct means by which the characteristics of the probability distribution can be discovered. The application of the expectation principle will require the individual to take the expected value of a Von Neumann–Morgenstern utility function; since this is usually assumed to be a polynomial in return (or wealth), then the expectation process will result in the individual's having to maximize an expected utility function which depends upon particular moments of the probability distribution. These are invariably confined to the mean and the variance. So each probability distribution of returns, for any portfolio, can be epitomized by those two magnitudes. On the hypothesis that the individual investor is a risk-averter, he will then wish to choose from the set of distributions those that promise the highest mean value of return for any given variance of return. Given the statistical definitions of the mean and the variance, it is relatively simple to discover the set of asset placings which will achieve that risk-constrained maximization. of the mean value of portfolio return. The outcome will be a mean/variance investment-opportunity frontier along which, for a given (mean/variance) combination, there is a unique allocation of wealth across some (maybe all) of the available assets. The Expected Utility function over, say, just the mean and the variance will result in the investor's choosing a combination of mean, variance along the frontier; that choice implies a choice of asset holdings for which, of course, there exists a formula connected to the mean (or variance) chosen and to the wealth constraint.

In effect, the expectation principle does provide a simple, neat and elegant route by which the almost infinite amount of expectational information contained in the probability distributions can be conflated. The editing or filtering device invoked by the expectation principle enables the whole gamut of probability distributions to be represented by two readily calculable magnitudes; and, by the same token, it obviates the necessity for the investor to construct the infinitely possible probability distribution of returns that are available to him from his wealth if he is permitted to allocate divisible units to any investment.

That is one argument in favour of the expectation principle, it must be conceded. However, there are many points that can be argued against it (*see* Chapter 1).

Perspective Theory makes no further demands on the technical knowledge and ingenuity of the individual investor than does the Expected Utility Theory. However, Perspective Theory requires the investor to process the probability distributions in an alternative way.

In Expected Utility Theory, it is supposed that the investor does know the probability distribution for any portfolio and not just for the returns per unit investment in each of the assets from which the global, portfolio returns must be constructed. Unless the individual asset returns are normally distributed, the portfolio distribution of returns need not possess the same probability density function as those of the individual asset returns. The derivations of portfolio probability distributions of returns from those for the individual asset returns is often only possible if non-linear restrictions are imposed on the combinations of assets held; otherwise the integrality condition, that the area under the probability density function be unity, cannot be satisfied.

The generally accepted procedure is, indeed, to assume that individual asset returns are normally distributed. Consequently, all portfolios will possess normal distributions.[1] For our purposes it is particularly apposite that a normal (and continuous)[2] distribution is selected for the returns per unit of investment in any asset. This is because it is symmetric about its mean, so that if it is assumed that all individual asset returns have *standard* normal distributions they possess gains and losses around a zero outcome.

Naturally, it is necessary to permit the random variables to possess differing variances, otherwise there is no effective action-choice to exercise the mind of the investor. The supposition that all distributions have a mean of zero makes it easier to locate the value of $\psi(.)$, the 'dis-utility' function.

The one disadvantage of the normal distribution is that it is not possible to derive an exact formula for its cumulative distribution function, $F(R)$. Recall that in Perspective Theory for gains $(R > 0)$ we need to operate in terms of $1 - F(R)$ and for losses $(R < 0)$ in terms of $F(R)|R \leqslant 0$. However, in applying Perspective Theory we can utilize the *general* representation of $F(R)$, namely:

$$F(R) = \Phi\left[\frac{R - \mu_R}{\sigma_R}\right] \qquad (4.1)$$

since we shall require only $F^1(R) \equiv f(R)$, where $f(R)$ is the probability density function of the random variable $R$.

Consider then the 'distribution functions' for gains/losses on any financial asset that has a mean of zero. Those distributions have been drawn in Figure 4.1. Imposed on the diagram are a sample of constant $\phi$ and $\psi$ (indifference) curves which exhibit the attitudes to outcomes and probabilities postulated in Chapter 3. If the individual investor's wealth happened to be £1 sterling, the distribution functions portrayed in Figure 4.1 would, naturally, indicate the prospect before him from his investing all of his wealth in the one asset.

Perspective Theory states that the investor takes a perspective on the available outcomes, runs his eye across them, keeping the gain and the loss outcomes segmented from each other initially. He acknowledges that at the most only one gain outcome is possible – likewise for loss outcomes – with only one type of outcome being

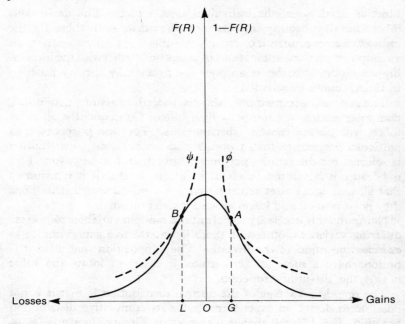

*Figure 4.1*

realizable. So he selects the most attractive gain outcome and the most unattractive loss outcome; then he weighs the one against other.

In terms of Figure 4.1 the maximum values of $\phi(.)$ and of $\psi(.)$ occur at points $A$ and $B$, respectively. At those points the two ascendancy functions have been maximized given the constraint that impinges on them via $F(R)$ and, implicitly, by the wealth constraint. At the points of maximum $\phi$ and $\psi$, the $\phi$ and $\psi$ indifference curves have slopes equal to $f(R)$.[3]

In Figure 4.1 I have assumed that the whole picture is one of symmetry since I have assumed that $\phi(.) = \psi(.)$. The individual decision-taker has to consider the range of distribution functions that are open to him (as he sees it himself, of course) and evaluate $(\phi, \psi)$. Clearly, he would endeavour to find a short-cut: such a method will sometimes be available.

To see how we can short-circuit the need to calculate every $F(R_i)$ and calculate out every $\phi^{\star}$ and $\psi^{\star}$, some specific forms for the ascendancy functions must be assumed. In effect, we shall let $\phi(.) = \psi(.)$, with:

$$\phi = 0.5 - e^{-G/2} + e^{\Pi/2} \qquad (4.2)$$

Here $G$ denotes gain and $\Pi$ is probability, defined as $1 - F(G)$. This form of $\phi$ encapsulates the essential ingredients of the ascendancy of the gain, probability characteristics of assets discussed previously. It expresses the investor's positive preferences for both higher gains and higher probability. There is no multiplicative term in $\Pi$ and $G$ as there might be: this only makes the analytical approach intractable, and a solution can be found only by means of a numerical computer model.

The probability density function for returns $(R_i)$ on any portfolio will be of this form:

$$f(R_i) = \frac{1}{\sigma_i \sqrt{2\text{Pi}}} e^{-\frac{1}{2}\left(\frac{R_i - \mu_i}{\sigma_i}\right)^2} \tag{4.3}$$

Here Pi is used for $f(R^i)$ rather than $\Pi$, which has been retained to indicate probability. In all $F(R)$ it has been assumed that $\mu_i = 0$. Hence equation (4.1) becomes:

$$F(R) = \phi\left(\frac{R}{\sigma_{R.}}\right) \tag{4.4}$$

Consider then the selection of $\phi^\star$ in Figure 4.1: that is, the selection of Point $A$. It is located where the slope of a $\phi$-indifference curve equals the derivative of $1 - F(R)$ with respect to $R$ (for $R > 0$). Hence it is found where (letting $G_i = R_i$ for $R_i > 0$):

$$\frac{1}{\sigma_i \sqrt{2\text{Pi}}} \exp\left[-\frac{1}{2}\left(\frac{G_i}{\sigma_i}\right)^2\right] = f(G_i) = \exp\left[-\frac{\Pi_i}{2} - \frac{G_i}{2}\right] \tag{4.5}$$

where exp is used for the Naperian $e$. Hence:

$$\exp\left[\frac{\Pi_i}{2}\right] = \exp\left[\frac{1}{2}\left(\frac{G_i}{\sigma_i}\right)^2 - \frac{G_i}{2}\right]\sigma_i \sqrt{2\text{Pi}} \tag{4.6}$$

Hence the maximum $\phi(.) = \phi^\star$ will be:

$$\phi^\star = 0.5 - \exp\left[-\frac{G_i}{2}\right] + \exp\left[\frac{1}{2}\left(\frac{G_i}{\sigma_i}\right)^2 - \frac{G_i}{2}\right]\sigma_i \sqrt{2\text{Pi}} \tag{4.7}$$

so the $G_i$ which maximizes $\phi(.)$ is obtained from:

$$\left(1 - \frac{2G_i}{\sigma_i^2}\right) = \frac{\exp\left(-\frac{1}{2}\left(\frac{G_i}{\sigma_i}\right)^2\right)}{\sigma_i \sqrt{2\ \text{Pi}}} \tag{4.8}$$

Since it has been assumed that $\phi(.) = \psi(.)$, $L_i$ at $\psi^\star$ must equal $G_i$ at $\phi^\star$. So we need concern ourselves only with $\phi^\star$ and its concomitant $G_i$. Now, let us postulate that:

$$P = P(\phi^\star, \psi^\star) = \alpha(\phi^\star)^2 - \beta\psi^\star; \alpha, \beta > 0 \qquad (4.9)$$

Given that $\phi^\star = \psi^\star$, $P$ is maximized when:

$$\phi = \frac{\beta}{2\alpha} \qquad (4.10)$$

For convenience let $\beta/2\alpha = 1.0$.

The maximum maximorum value of $\phi^\star$ when $P(.)$ is maximized will then simply be as follows (letting $\phi^\star$ in equation (4.7) equal 1):

$$\exp\left[\tfrac{1}{2}\left(\frac{G_i}{\sigma_i}\right)^2 - \left(\frac{G_i}{2}\right)\right]\sigma_i \sqrt{2\text{Pi}} - \exp\left[-\frac{G_i}{2}\right] = 0.5 \qquad (4.11)$$

Thus, when equations (4.8) and (4.11) are solved they will produce the values of $G_i$ and $\sigma_i$ which maximize $P$.

Now, from equation (4.8) it can also be deduced at the optimum portfolio that:

$$f(G_I) = \left(1 - \frac{2G_i}{\sigma_i^2}\right) \qquad (4.12)$$

Once $G_i$ and $\sigma_i$ are discovered, equation (4.12) permits us to locate the *ajs*, that is the gains per unit of investment in each of the $j$ assets at $f(G_i)$. The conditions for a maximum value of $\phi(.)$ defined in equation (4.5) enable us to deduce the value of $1 - F(G_i)$.

So, in the simplifying conditions assumed here, the general solution to the optimum portfolio requires the investor to solve these two equations simultaneously for $G_i$ and $\sigma_i$:

$$1 - \frac{2G_i}{\sigma_i^2} = \frac{\exp\left(-\tfrac{1}{2}\left(\frac{G_i}{\sigma_i}\right)^2\right)}{\sigma_i \sqrt{2\text{Pi}}} \qquad (4.13)$$

$$2\exp\left[\tfrac{1}{2}\left(\frac{G_i}{\sigma_i}\right)^2 - \frac{G_i}{2}\right]\sigma_i \sqrt{2\text{Pi}} - 2\exp\left[-\frac{G_i}{2}\right] = 1 \qquad (4.14)$$

Then, given $G_i$ and $\sigma_i$, the portfolio allocation is achieved by solving simultaneously these equations:

$$G = \Sigma a_j X_j \qquad (4.15)$$
$$\sigma^2 = \Sigma \sigma_j^2 X_j^2 \qquad (4.16)$$
$$W = \Sigma X_j \qquad (4.17)$$

Here: $W$ is wealth; $X_j$ is the value of the holding of asset $j$; $a$ is the return per unit of investment in asset $j$ at $f(G_i)$ and $\sigma_j^2$ is the variance of the return per unit of investment in asset $j$.

Quite evidently in these circumstances a multi-asset portfolio can be held. Any degree of asset-diversification will be increased if $\psi(.) \neq \phi(.)$ of course: there would then be an equation for $L_i$. Because of the assumption that $\phi(.) = \psi(.)$, the normality properties of the probability density functions mean that, effectively, choice over ($\phi^\star$, $\psi^\star$) has become a choice over ($G^\star$, $L^\star$), with the $G - L$ frontier being linear.

Let us now consider a specific portfolio problem. It is usually the case that in the treatment of portfolio selection, as special examples, attention is focused on 'money and bonds' models or on models with money and two risky assets, such as short-term and long-term bonds. Let us examine the simple one of money ($M$) and bonds ($B$).

In this situation, if it is posited that money promised neither gains nor losses (recall our assumptions about expected inflation), holding money offers a zero value of $\phi$ and $\psi$ and hence of $P$. In essence, the 'net advantage' of holding wealth in the form of money balances is to place the investor on what might be labelled his origin $P$-indifference curve in ($\phi$, $\psi$) space.

Holding a bond promises the possibility of gains and losses (of positive and negative yields if one prefers to think of asset choice in these terms). It may be supposed that the bond possesses a standard normal distribution with a mean of zero, and a variance of $\sigma_B^2$. Retaining all of the assumptions made hitherto about $\phi(.)$, $\psi(.)$, and their equivalence, we find the investor confronted by a choice of portfolio based implicitly on a choice of $G^\star$ against $L^\star$. The $G^\star = f(L^\star)$ frontier is linear: it commences now, however, at the origin of the Cartesian diagram in $G$ and $L$, because of the presence of money with its assumed attributes of zero monetary outcomes. Its maximum point has to be the ($G,L$) that is generated by the allocation of all of wealth to the bond.

By trading some of the bond for money the individual will be trading off gain against loss, hope against fear; substituting a smaller $\psi$ for a smaller $\phi$. Yet that might be his preference given $P = P(\phi, \psi)$. He might be so risk-averse that he does not wish to take the extreme step of placing 'all his eggs in one basket', with the promise of a high gain or the threat of a possible severe loss that could reduce his wealth to a disastrous level.

In that case where $P$ is, say, of the form $\alpha\phi - \beta(\psi)^2$, the investor might well protect himself by selecting a $G$ (equals $L$) such as $OA$ in Figure 4.2.

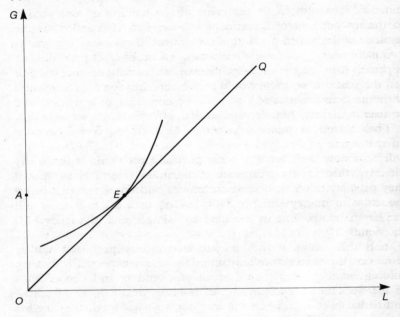

*Figure 4.2*

The $(G,L)$ combination selected will imply the combination of money and bonds held. So that, as hitherto, $G^\star$ will imply $f(G)$, which will imply a value of the per unit returns on money and bonds (that is, specify the relevant state of nature, $j$). Hence:

$$G = a_{Mj}x_M + a_{Bj}x_B; a_{Mj} = 0 \tag{4.18}$$

$$\sigma^2 = \sigma_B^2 x_B^2 \Rightarrow \sigma = \sigma_B x_B \tag{4.19}$$

$$W = x_M + x_B \tag{4.20}$$

In this special instance, with $\sigma$ dependent only upon the holding of bonds, the value of bond holdings can be determined merely from the variance implicitly selected, or from $G$. If those values are too small to be consistent with $x_B = W$, some money balances must be held, their value being obtained as the residual from the wealth constraint.

What structure do the asset demand equations take on? How will 'money bonds' choice be affected by changes in wealth or in the characteristics of bonds? In the probabilistic variant of Perspective Theory it is not feasible in principle to deduce the asset demands and hence the asset demand equations, by carrying out the procedure of choosing the set of $x$s directly that maximize the perspective function. This is because the derivative of $G$ (and of $L$) with respect to the $x_i$ cannot be obtained since it depends upon the 'state of nature', which is implicitly to be chosen, via the selection of the two pairs of $(G, \Pi_G)$ and $(L, \Pi_L)$ for each set of $x$s. The 'top level' approach to solving for the $x$s has to be adopted; only by deduction can the portfolio allocation be determined. That is not the situation with the credibility index version of Perspective Theory, as will be seen in the later part of this chapter.

The holding of bonds will depend, from the deduction method, on the variables considered in the multi-asset case. That is, they will be affected, implicitly, by the properties of $P(.)$, $\phi(.)$, $\psi(.)$ and directly by the variances of the returns on the assets, the gains/losses they promise per unit of investment over states of nature and by the scalar variable, wealth.

The solution of the actual holdings of the $x$s derived from $G$, $L$, $\sigma^2$ and $W$ naturally does not portray the demand equations *per se*, only their *values* in the expectational and wealth circumstances. However, they indicate the variables that impinge directly on asset choice; and they can be supplemented, as above, by the properties of the behavioural functions that lead to the choice of $G$, $L$, ... and hence to the $x$s. The solution for the value of the $x$s will, that is, only produce values for the $x$s and values that depend upon $\sigma_i^2$, some $a_{ij}$ and upon wealth. Nevertheless they will exhibit the usual aggregation condition over those variables, namely Cournot and Engel: the coefficients on the characteristics of the assets summing to zero, the sum of the coefficients on wealth summing to unity.

Should there be a *ceteris paribus* increase in wealth, how will this affect the investor's choice of portfolio? If it is assumed that the increase in wealth is not large enough to influence $\psi(.)$ or $P(.)$ then, with $\phi(.)$ and $\psi(.)$ still identical, the choice of portfolio remains as one over a transformed $P(.)$, one over $(G,L)$. The (optimum) frontier connecting those two magnitudes stays linear; an increase in wealth merely extends that frontier in a north-easterly direction in $(G,L)$ space.

The maximum $(G,L)$ occurs, under my assumptions, when all of the wealth is placed into the asset that possesses the highest variance of per unit returns. In the money-bonds world the frontier extends beyond $Q$ in Figure 4.2. With the increase in wealth having been supposed not to be large enough to affect the investor's degree of risk-aversion, all of the extra wealth must be held in the form of money balances. In terms of Figure 4.2, the optimum point, $E$, does not alter.

In the terminology of the orthodox, Expected Utility model, the investor exhibits constant risk-aversion and increasing relative risk-aversion. However, those two forms of risk-aversion cannot be measured in the orthodox way, via the Pratt–Arrow method (see Pratt (1964)), in view of the fact that the investor's 'utility' function is defined separately over gains/losses, is related to both outcome and probability, and is not dependent only on returns/level of wealth. These two measures of risk-aversion are defined as:

$$ARA = \frac{-U''(R)}{U'(R)} \; ; \text{ and } RRA = \frac{-U''(R)R}{U'(R)} \tag{4.21}$$

or

$$ARA = \frac{-U''(W)}{U'(W)}; \text{ and } RRA = \frac{-U''(W)W}{U'(W)} \tag{4.22}$$

where $ARA$ and $RRA$ are, respectively, absolute and relative risk-aversion defined over 'the' *actual* (ex post) utility function $U = U(R)$ or $U = U(W)$.

Nevertheless they have the two implications I have drawn above. Thus, if $ARA$ is constant (with respect to $R$ or to $W$) this means that as wealth increases the total amount of risk assumed by the investor remains fixed. There risk is assessed by the appropriate risk-characteristic that emerges from application of the expectation principle to the actual utility function; in the majority of instances, as commented previously, that characteristic will be the variance of returns or of wealth. With constant absolute risk aversion, $\sigma^2$, the risk of the whole portfolio for a given placement of wealth across the assets will remain constant as investable wealth rises; and with increasing relative risk-aversion the ratio between $\sigma^2$ and $W$ must fall as $W$ increases.

If the increase in wealth is large, how large 'large' needs to be cannot be told *a priori*, the individual's attitude to losses and hence his risk-aversion will be reduced. For any allocation of wealth, say, wealth held completely in bonds, the increase in wealth will cause a mean-preserving spread in the possible returns: at each $F(R)$, gains/losses will be higher except at the mean of zero. So the gains/losses from allocating the whole of wealth to bonds shifts from the $AZB$ distribution function to one such as that epitomized by $A'ZB'$ in Figure 4.3.

The reduced aversion to losses is likely to operate through both less weight being placed on losses in $\psi(.)$ and to less relative importance being assigned to $\psi^\star$ in $P(.)$. It is feasible, therefore, that this transformation of $\psi(.)$ could, when $\psi(.)$ is maximized, lead to a lower loss being selected than was hitherto the case with the $\psi(.)$ for the original wealth level. The lower weight attached to $\psi^\star$ in

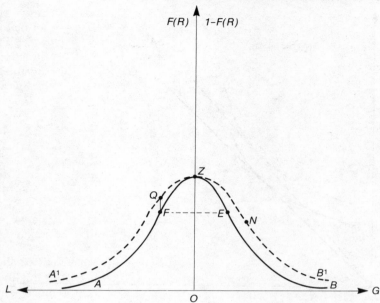

*Figure 4.3*

$P(.)$ would the amplify the pull of the higher prospective gain that could be made on bonds consequent upon the scale effect engendered by the increase in wealth. Suppose, for example, that the translation of $\psi(.)$ is such that the loss chosen, with its associated probability level that maximizes $\psi(.)$ under the higher level of wealth, happens to be identical to the relevant loss level at the old wealth level. This would, for example, lead to $Q$ being the point of maximum $\psi(.)$ along $A'B'$ if it is assumed that the original position was $F$. Now, however, $G$ at max $\phi(.)$ must be higher than hitherto: the $(G,L)$ frontier, although retaining its linearity, lies above that for the original wealth level (except, of course, at the origin).

The shift in the perspective function will amplify the switch in favour of gains. Consequently, a higher value of $L$ could be selected for the new portfolio under increased wealth, because the investor's willingness to take on losses has increased. The higher the loss he is prepared to assume, however, the higher must be the gains he can expect, via the positive relationship that prevails between gains and losses on the optimum investment frontier. Consider then Figure 4.4, where the initial optimum point is $E$ on $OA$: after the increase in wealth I assume that it is located at $Z$ on $OA'$. Since $G^\star$ has

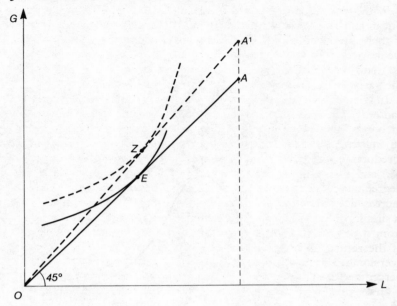

*Figure 4.4*

increased, so too must $\sigma^2$ and, hence, $x_B$ must have increased because $\sigma_B^2$ has not been assumed to change; only the portfolio variance of bonds has increased with the expansion of wealth. It cannot be stated *a priori* what will happen to the share of bonds in wealth. The new $P(.)$ needs to be specified. Note that in Perspective Theory there is no precise relationship between the two frontiers, $OA$ and $OA'$. Thus, a doubling of wealth will not be sufficient information to state that $L$ and $G$ have increased proportionately by a factor $y$. This is because the choices of the maximum $G$ and $L$ arise out of the maximization of $\phi(.)$ and $\psi(.)$, respectively. I have postulated that the maximum value of the 'new' $\psi(.)$ will produce the same value of $L$, as previously, when all wealth is allocated to bonds. However, although $G$ will increase it cannot be stipulated that its increase will equal, say, the increase in wealth. Since there is no direct relationship between the end-points of the two frontiers and wealth, the same is true, *mutatis mutandis*, to all intermediate points.

A *ceteris paribus* increase in the mean-preserving spread of the returns on bonds will, naturally, affect the distribution of returns on the 'all wealth held in bonds' portfolio in the way illustrated in Figure 4.3.

With unchanged $\phi(.)$ and $\psi(.)$, and the $(G,L)$ frontier will remain linear and will be extended in a north-easterly direction, just as if there had been a *ceteris paribus* increase in wealth. The fact that we have $\phi(.) = \psi(.)$ and no alteration in $P(.)$ results in $G^\star$ $(= L^\star)$ and $\sigma^2$ being the same as they were prior to the increase in the variance of returns per unit of investment in bonds $(\sigma_B^2)$.

In view of the increase in that variance, the portfolio variance can only remain constant if the investor is placing less of his wealth in bonds than previously. In this two asset, money-bonds world, an increase in the riskiness of bonds will lead, *ceteris paribus*, to a reduction in the holding of bonds. If $\psi(.)$ had been different from $\phi(.)$ and to the extent that the investor was more risk-averse, the degree of reduction in the holding of bonds as their riskiness increased would have been more substantial. The reason for that is simple; given a fixed $P(.)$, the increased unattractiveness that arises from a pair of $(L,\Pi_L)$, an increase in the mean-preserving spread of the return on bonds increases $L$ for given $F(L)$. The increased aversion to loss now increases $L$ when $\psi(.)$ is maximized by a greater percentage than it increases $G$ when $\phi(.)$ is maximized.

In the preceding paragraphs we have considered a model composed of one riskless and one risky asset. Most of what has been said applies *mutatis mutandis* to the situation where the alternative financial claims available for purchase consist of a riskless and two risky assets. The only comment I might add to those previously made is that (with $\phi(.) = \psi(.)$ still) the investor now has to solve two equations to determine the risky assets, and a residual equation, that for wealth, to determine the best holding of the riskless asset, 'money'. The equations will be of this form (assuming independence between asset returns):

$$G = a_{1j}x_1 + a_{2j}x_2 \qquad (4.23)$$
$$\sigma^2 = \sigma_1^2 x_1^2 + \sigma_2^2 x_2^2 \qquad (4.24)$$

with '1' and '2' denoting the two risky assets.

We consider now the question of asset choice in Perspective Theory when the probability density function of the individual asset returns is replaced by a credibility index, indicating the strength of belief in the occurrence of the particular outcomes.

Again, in order to derive some tangible, analytical results concerning asset selection rather than just to state possibilities, it is necessary to put some specific detail into the theory. Let it be assumed then, for the sake of this formal objective, that the credibility functions $\theta(.)$ for the per unit returns on the available financial claims possess these simple linear forms:

$$\theta_i^g = \alpha_i - \beta_i g_i \tag{4.25}$$

$$\theta_i^l = \gamma_i - \delta_i l_i \tag{4.26}$$

Here: $\alpha_i$, $\beta_i$, $\gamma_i$ and $\delta_i$ are positive parameters; the subscript $i$ refers to asset $i$; $g$ and $l$ denote gains, losses, respectively per unit of return; capital $G$ and $L$ will be used to represent the portfolio magnitudes of gain and loss.

Naturally, these are special credibility functions, *ex hypothesi*. They place the weight of evidence on the likelihood of losses and gains concentrated around zero. At the portfolio level, for any set of asset placings, $x_i$, they permit us to deduce the following relationships:

$$G = (\alpha/\beta)_i' x_i - (1/\beta)_i' x_i \theta_G \tag{4.27}$$

$$L = (\gamma/\delta)_i' x_i - (1/\delta)_i' x_i \theta_L \tag{4.28}$$

In these equations I have moved into matrix notation since the credibility index variant of Perspective Theory does allow us to operate at a more general level. Thus, for example: $(\alpha/\beta)_i'$ is the row vector of $(\alpha/\beta)_i$ and is $1{\times}n$; $x_i$ is the $n{\times}1$ vector of (values of) asset holdings of the available $x$, constrained to be equal to wealth; and $\theta_G$ is the credibility index for the appropriate value of $G$. Equations (4.27) and (4.28) are just equations (4.25) and (4.26) summed over $x_i$, that is, summed laterally in $(G,\theta)$ space, $G$ denoting the horizontal axis of the Cartesian diagram.

For any prescribed portfolio there will clearly be a credibility function for gains, $\theta_G = \theta_G(x_i)$ and for losses, $\theta_L = \theta_L(x_i)$. The logical procedure by which the investor has to determine his optimum portfolio means that he cannot select, directly, that set of $x$s that will maximize the value of his perspective function for his given level of wealth. He first of all, in principle, has to evaluate for *any set* of placings, the maximum value of $\phi(.)$ and of $\psi(.)$, where each ascendancy function is maximized subject to the wealth level and, respectively, to the credibility function, $\theta = \theta(G)$ and $\theta = \theta(L)$, characterized by equations (4.27) and (4.28). The pairs of $(\phi_{\max}, \psi_{\max})$ are then ranked via $P(.)$; or the pairs of $(G^\star, L^\star)$ at $\phi_{\max}$ and $\psi_{\max}$ are compared via a transformed $P(.)$, if such a translation is legitimate.

Therefore, for any given portfolio within his wealth constraint, the investor calculates the maximum value of $\phi$ and of $\psi$. Let us postulate the following ascendancy functions:

$$\phi = \theta_G G + G \tag{4.29}$$

$$\psi = \theta_L L^2 \tag{4.30}$$

It is necessary to assume that $\phi(.)$ does differ from $\psi(.)$ in this variant of the Perspective Theory portfolio model to prevent the matrix of coefficients on $x_i$ being singular when we come to solve for the optimum vector of asset holdings.

When $\theta_G$ is chosen to permit $\phi$ to be maximized, for given $x_i$, subject to equation (4.27) it is discovered that:

$$\theta_G = \frac{(\alpha/\beta)'_i x_i - (1/\beta_i)' x_i}{2(1/\beta_i)' x_i} \qquad (4.31)$$

As a consequence, the $G$ that maximizes $\phi$, subject that is to $\theta_G = f(G)$ given by equation (4.31), is:

$$G = (\alpha/\beta)'_i x_i - \left[ \frac{(\alpha/\beta)'_i x_i - (1/\beta_i)' x_i}{2} \right] \qquad (4.32)$$

From equations (4.28) and (4.30):

$$L = \frac{2}{3}(\gamma/\delta)' x_i \qquad (4.32a)$$

The corresponding expressions for $\phi^\star$ and $\psi^\star$ are:

$$\phi^\star = \frac{x'_i A x_i + x'_i B x_i + 2x' \Omega x}{4(1/\beta_i)' x_i} \qquad (4.32b)$$

$$\psi^\star = \frac{4}{27} \frac{(\gamma/\delta)'_i x_i}{(1/\delta_i)' x_i} \, [x'_i \Gamma x] \qquad (4.32c)$$

where: $A = (\alpha/\beta)_i (\alpha/\beta)'_i; \; B = (1/\beta)_i (1/\beta)'_i$
$\Omega = (1/\beta)_i (\alpha/\beta)'_i;$ and $\Gamma = (1/\delta)_i (1/\delta)'_i$

The non-linearity in $x_i$ that occurs in both $\phi^\star$ and $\psi^\star$ makes it impossible to derive an analytical solution for the sets of $x$s of the $(\phi^\star, \psi^\star)$ frontier and in 'the' portfolio that maximizes the perspective index. To proceed with the generation of such a solution some further simplifying assumptions must be made. The obvious candidates concern the parameters in the $\theta$ functions. Let all $\alpha_i = 2$, and also all $\gamma_i = 2$ (so that $\bar\theta$ is normalized at two rather than one, as it was in Chapter 3). On the hypothesis that:

$$P = a\phi^2 - b\psi \qquad (4.33)$$

the Lagrangean for the minimization of $\psi$ with respect to $x_i$ subject to $\phi^\star$ and wealth is:

$$\mathscr{L} = \frac{4}{27} x' \Delta x + \lambda_1 (\frac{3}{4}(1/\beta)_i' x_i - \phi^\star) + \lambda_2 (i' x_i - W) \qquad (4.34)$$

with: $\Delta = (1/\delta)_i (1/\delta)'_i$ and $i'$ a $1 \times n$ vector of ones. The first-order conditions reveal that:

$$\left.\begin{array}{r} \dfrac{8}{27}\,\Delta x_i - \dfrac{3}{4}(\mathrm{I}/\beta)_i\lambda_\mathrm{I} - \lambda_2 i = \mathrm{o} \\[2mm] \dfrac{3}{4}(\mathrm{I}/\beta)'_i x_i = \phi^\star \\[2mm] i'x_i = W \end{array}\right\} \qquad (4.35)$$

It is usual to write this in matrix form as:

$$\begin{bmatrix} \dfrac{8}{27}\Delta & \dfrac{3}{4}(\mathrm{I}/\beta)_i & i \\[2mm] \Big(\dfrac{3}{4}\Big)(\mathrm{I}/\beta)'_i & \mathrm{o} & \mathrm{o} \\[2mm] i' & \mathrm{o} & \mathrm{o} \end{bmatrix} \begin{bmatrix} x \\[2mm] \lambda_\mathrm{I} \\[2mm] \lambda_2 \end{bmatrix} = \begin{bmatrix} \mathrm{o} \\[2mm] \phi^\star \\[2mm] W \end{bmatrix} \qquad (4.36)$$

This partitioning is the neatest to adopt since the aim is to find an expression for $x_i$ in terms of $\phi^\star$ and $W$ which can be inserted into the formula for $\psi^\star$. However, it is not a feasible proposition in this model, because the block inversion of the coefficient matrix in equation (4.36) requires the matrix $8/27\Delta$ to be non-singular. However, it is not only a symmetric but also a singular matrix.

It is possible, in fact, to re-partition the matrix of coefficients, which I shall label $M$. However, nothing is to be gained by re-partitioning $M$ in (4.36) and block inverting it. If $M$ is $(n + 2)$ x $(n + 2)$ then, in general terms:

$$x = M_{n+1}\phi^\star + M_{n+2}W \qquad (4.37)$$

where: $M_{n+1}$ and $M_{n+2}$ are the first $n$ elements in the $n + 1$ and $n + 2$ columns of $M^{-1}$. Substitution of equation (4.37) into the equation for $\psi^\star$, namely equation (4.35) adjusted for $\gamma_i = 2$ yields:

$$\psi^\star = \frac{8}{27}\,x'\,\Gamma x :$$

$$\therefore \psi^\star = \frac{8}{27}\,(M_{n+1}\phi^\star + M_{n+2}W)'\Gamma(M_{n+1}\phi^\star + M_{n+2}W) \quad (4.38)$$

This provides the individual investor with the best terms upon which he can 'trade' $\phi^\star$ for $\psi^\star$. As is seen, that frontier is non-linear being a quadratic in $\phi^\star$. The frontier between $\phi^\star$ and $\psi^\star$ can be either convex or concave: making the working assumption that there are only three assets over which the investor may spread his wealth enables us to unscramble $M_{n+1}$ and $M_{n+2}$ in a way that permits us to see that the sign of the first derivative of $\phi^\star = f(\psi^\star)$ is positive, with the sign of $f''(.)$ probably negative.

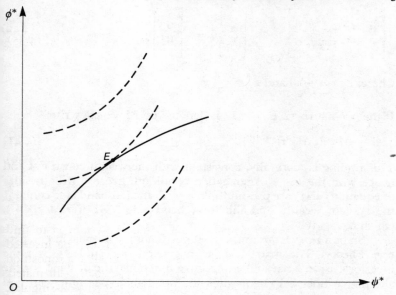

*Figure 4.5*

In essence, the ascendancy frontier over which the individual chooses in order to maximize his perspective index is likely to be of the shape portrayed in Figure 4.5. The investor now selects the point $E$ via his perspective function; accordingly, since he has selected *the* $\phi^\star$ out of the available set, he has also determined the best vector of $x$s, the $x_i$, which are derived from equation (4.37) by simple arithmetic calculation, with $\phi^\star$, $W$ and the expectational (credibility function) attributes of the assets already being pre-determined.

However, what about the demand equations *per se* for the optimum set of $x$s, rather than the values of the items in the set? In this version of Perspective Theory those demand equations can be obtained directly, and by following the conventional path. Thus the investor in this presentation chooses $x_i$ to maximize $P = P(\phi^\star, \psi^\star)$ subject to $\phi^\star$, $\psi^\star$ and $W$.

In formal terms the Lagrangean is:[4]

$$\mathscr{L} = (\tfrac{9}{16})ax'Bx - (\tfrac{4}{27})bx'\Gamma x + \lambda_i(i'x_i - W) \qquad (4.39)$$

The first-order conditions for a maximum of $\mathscr{L}$ reveal that:

$$\begin{bmatrix} (z_1B - z_2\Gamma) & i \\ i'' & o \end{bmatrix} \begin{bmatrix} x \\ \hline \lambda_1 \end{bmatrix} = \begin{bmatrix} o \\ \hline W \end{bmatrix} \qquad (4.40)$$

where: $z_1 = (\frac{9}{16})\, a$ and $z_2 = (\frac{4}{27})b$.

If the $nxn$ matrix $(z_1B - z_2\Gamma)$ is denoted by $M$ we can write:[5]

$$x_i = M^{-1}i(i'M^{-1}i)^{-1}(W) \qquad (4.41)$$

This finding is, naturally, consistent with the wealth constraint and hence with the Engel Aggregation condition, because if both sides of equation (4.41) are pre-multiplied by $i'$, the left hand side contains the sum of wealth, and the right hand side $(i'M^{-1}i)(i'M^{-1}i)(W)$ which equals $W$.

$x_i$ can be a $1xn$ vector: multi-asset portfolios are rational in Perspective Theory. The matrix $M$ is, in general, invertible. Given the investor's ascendancy and perspective functions, the demand for the alternative financial claims depends upon their per unit gain and loss characteristics, as epitomized in their credibility functions, and by the level of the scalar variable, wealth. Cournot Aggregation must hold *ex definitione*, as it has been seen that Engel Aggregation does.

However, these notions can be examined in more detail and the effects of changes in asset characteristics and wealth upon the investor's optimum portfolio can be investigated by considering the Marginal Advantage curves for the assets. These lie behind the demand equations *per se*, and represent the partial derivatives of the perspective function with respect to each of the $x$s unconstrained by wealth. Because of the latter property the Marginal Advantage curves are easier to unscramble than the demand equations, but to make full use of them I do have to introduce wealth, even if only pictorially.

One of the usual models employed to highlight the properties of the theory of portfolio selection comprises money and two risky assets. A model of this modest dimension will enable us to deduce exactly, the demand equations of the individual investor.

The Marginal Advantage curves are provided by these equations:

$$\frac{\partial P}{\partial x} = (z_1B - z_2\Gamma)x_i \qquad (4.42)$$

The Marginal Advantage of holding money $(x_1)$ will be zero in this framework. The Marginal Advantage ($MA$) of the two risky assets, assets two and three, will be:

$$MA_2 = (z_1/\beta_2^2 - z_2/\delta_2^2)x_2 + (z_1/\beta_2\beta_3 - z_2/\delta_2\delta_3)x_3 \qquad (4.43)$$

$$MA_3 = (z_1/\beta_3\beta_2 - z_2/\delta_3\delta_2)x_2 + (z_1/\beta_3^2 - z_2/\delta_3^2)x_3 \qquad (4.44)$$

The advantage, at the margin, of transferring one unit of wealth from, say, money into asset two depends upon the existing holding of asset three. The Marginal Advantage of increasing the holding of either of the risky assets, for a given value of the holding of the other, will fall only if the coefficients $(z_1/\beta_i^2 - z_2/\delta_i^2)$ are negative. The occurrence of that outcome would reflect the effect of the two influences on the benefits of purchasing an additional unit of currency's worth of an asset; namely, the gain at the margin compared with the loss (operating via $\beta_i$, $\delta_i$) and the aversion to overall (portfolio) loss relative to total gain, as reflected in the coefficients $z_1$, $z_2$. It will not always follow, therefore, that increased holdings of any asset imply diminishing Marginal Advantage; in a mean/variance framework it might be found that that is so. Sir John Hicks (1967) has argued that such a result in mean–variance analysis should be expected if asset diversification is to occur, rather than the 'corner' solution where wealth is held in one or a tiny number of assets. However, the prevalence of diminishing Marginal Advantage is not inevitable even in a mean/variance context.

For a unit value holding of either asset two or asset three, the Marginal Advantage curves of the two assets will be linear, of course, and if they do also exhibit diminishing Marginal Advantage they will be of the kind illustrated in Figure 4.6. Both 'curves' have the same intercept on the vertical axis. The wealth constraint would result in a portfolio of $OZ$ of $x_2$ and $ZQ$ of $x_3$.

However, because $MA_i$ depends upon $x_j$ as well as $x_i$, it is not strictly correct to construct Figure 4.6 on the *ceteris paribus* hypothesis that, for $MA_i$, $x_j$ is fixed. Should that have been true then the Marginal Advantage of both $x_2$ and $x_3$ could never have attained a value of zero; in which event, no money could have been retained in the optimum portfolio. The asset dependency of the Marginal Advantage curves for the risky assets does not ultimately entail the existence of a three asset, with money, portfolio.

This can be demonstrated quite simply. If the Marginal Advantage equations for assets two and three are taken, it can be deduced that they can only simultaneously be zero if the coefficient matrix on $(x_2, x_3)$ in equations (4.43) and (4.44) is singular. All assets held in the optimum portfolio must *ex definitione* possess the same value of Marginal Advantage. The Marginal Advantage on both assets two and three cannot be pushed to zero, the Marginal Advantage of money, unless the two assets are intrinsically indistinguishable

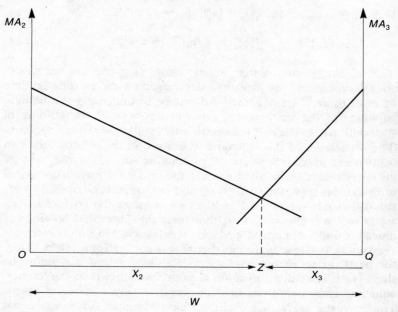

*Figure 4.6*

from money.

Let us assume that all three assets are risky and derive their demand equations. These are obtained from:

$$\begin{bmatrix} (z_1 B - z_2 \Gamma) & i \\ \hline i'' & o \end{bmatrix} \begin{bmatrix} x_i \\ \hline \lambda_1 \end{bmatrix} = \begin{bmatrix} o \\ \hline W \end{bmatrix} \tag{4.45}$$

The matrix of coefficients is written thus:

$$\begin{bmatrix} a_{11} & a_{12} & a_{13} & 1 \\ a_{21} & a_{22} & a_{23} & 1 \\ a_{31} & a_{32} & a_{33} & 1 \\ 1 & 1 & 1 & o \end{bmatrix} \tag{4.46}$$

where: $a_{12} = a_{21}; a_{13} = a_{31}; a_{23} = a_{32}$ and:

$$a_{11} = z_1/\beta_1^2 - z_2/\delta_1^2; \quad a_{12} = z_1/\beta_1\beta_2 - z_2/\delta_1\delta_2;$$

$$a_{13} = z_1/\beta_1\beta_3 - z_2/\delta_1\delta_3; \quad a_{22} = z_1/\beta_2^2 - z_2/\delta_2^2;$$

$$a_{23} = z_1/\delta_2\delta_3 - z_2/\delta_2\delta_3; \quad a_{33} = z_1/\beta_3^2 - z_2/\delta_3^2.$$

The demand equations are:

$$x_1 = \Delta^{-1} [a_{12}(a_{23}-a_{33}) - a_{22}(a_{13}-a_{33}) + a_{32}(a_{13}-a_{23})]W \qquad (4.47)$$
$$x_2 = \Delta^{-1} [a_{11}(a_{23}-a_{33}) - a_{21}(a_{13}-a_{33}) + a_{31}(a_{13}-a_{23})]W \qquad (4.48)$$
$$x_3 = \Delta^{-1} [a_{11}(a_{22}-a_{32}) - a_{21}(a_{12}-a_{32}) + a_{31}(a_{12}-a_{22})]W \qquad (4.49)$$

Here $\Delta^{-1}$ is the inverse of the determinant of (4.46).

Given $\Delta$ it can be seen that the wealth constraint is, indeed, binding; Engel Aggregation holds, with the sum of the coefficients on wealth, hence the sum of the $x$s, amounting to $W$. To examine the Cournot Aggregation condition and to investigate the effect of *ceteris paribus* alterations in the characteristics of the assets upon the composition of the portfolio we can differentiate equations (4.47) to (4.49), but these issues can be handled more neatly and transparently if we make the simplifying assumption that only two risky assets can be held, since we have shown that more than two assets, indeed $n$ assets, can rationally be held in the investor's portfolio.

Assume that asset three, perhaps equities, cannot be selected in the portfolio and the individual is confronted by a choice between short- and long-term government bonds, assets one and two. The equations reduce to:

$$x_1 = \frac{(a_{12} - a_{22})W}{a_{12} - a_{11} + a_{21} - a_{22}} \qquad (4.50)$$

$$x_2 = \frac{(a_{21} - a_{11})W}{a_{12} - a_{11} + a_{21} - a_{22}} \qquad (4.51)$$

Let us consider the *ceteris paribus* effect of a change in $\beta_1$ on portfolio composition. It is discovered that:

$$\frac{\partial(x_1/W)}{\partial\beta_1} = \frac{-(z_1/\beta_1^2\beta_2)D - (a_{12}-a_{22})(\partial D/\partial\beta_1)}{D^2} \qquad (4.52)$$

$$\frac{\partial(x_2/W)}{\partial\beta_1} = \frac{(2z_1/\beta_1^3 - 2z_1/\beta_1^2\beta_2)D - (a_{12}-a_{11})(\partial D/\partial\beta_1)}{D^2} \qquad (4.53)$$

where D is the denominator of equations (4.50) and (4.51). Summing equations (4.52) and (4.53) it is found that they do add to zero.[6]

Naturally, it is discovered that the Cournot Aggregation condition is satisfied for the other (implicit) asset characteristics, namely $\beta_2$, $\delta_1$ and $\delta_2$. What, however, will be the sign of $\partial(x_1/W)/\partial\beta_1$? Will the share of $x_1$ in the portfolio increase if $\beta_1$ falls? That is the outcome that is intuitively to be expected; the reduction in $\beta_1$ means that the credibility of every gain per unit of investment in asset one has increased. At the margin its gain/loss characteristic has improved: at the margin the gain on the portfolio can be increased by switching funds into asset one. That argument is too restricted; and it leads to the impression that $x_1$ will increase automatically. Whether it does or not depends upon: the gain credibility function for asset two; the gain and loss credibility functions for both assets; and, possibly, the comparative weights associated with gains and losses in the Perspective Function.

For the two-asset example, we have:

$$\frac{\partial x_1}{\partial \beta_1} \gtreqless 0 \text{ as: } z_1\left(\frac{1}{\beta_2^3} - \frac{1}{\beta_1^2 \beta_2}\right) - z_2\left(\frac{1}{\delta_1^2 \beta_2} + \frac{1}{\delta_2^2 \beta_2} - \frac{1}{\delta_1 \delta_2 \beta_1}\right) \gtreqless 0 \quad (4.54)$$

with $z_1 = 9a/16$ and $z_2 = 4b/27$.

Thus: the sufficient conditions for $\partial(x_1/W)/\partial\beta_1$ to be negative are:

$$\beta_1 < \beta_2 \text{ and } \frac{\beta_1}{\beta_2}\left(\frac{\delta_2^2 + \delta_1^2}{\delta_1 \delta_2}\right) > 1 \quad (4.55)$$

If $\beta_1 < \beta_2$ it must follow that $\delta_1 < \delta_2$, otherwise, over both gains and losses, asset one would dominate asset two. By the condition $\beta_1 < \beta_2$, the coefficient $(\delta_2^2 + \delta_1^2)/\delta_1\delta_2$ must be less than unity for the second inequality in (4.55) to be valid. However, $\delta_1 < \delta_2$ will mean that it is greater than that required figure. Hence, it is possible for $x_1/W$ to increase, stay constant, or fall, when there is a *ceteris paribus* increase in $\beta_1$.

The gain characteristic of asset one has improved. Nevertheless, this need not lead to an automatic increase in $x_1$. The reduction in $\beta_1$ will raise the value attained by the ascendancy function $\phi(.)$. Increasing the holding of $x_1$ will, compared with holding asset two, increase the value of the $\psi$ index. In principle, at any given $\psi^*$ it is now possible for the investor to extract a higher $\phi^*$ from his original portfolio, because of the improvement in the promised gains from asset one. Accordingly, he could reduce his holding of asset one, still increase his $\phi^*$ and also reduce his $\psi^*$.

There is present here standard preference effects analogous to the familiar income and substitution effects. These effects are for all intents and purposes indistinguishable from the wealth and substitution effects that prevail in mean/variance or Expected Utility models of asset choice.

The improvement in the gain credibility function for asset one is tantamount to a wealth effect, envisaged as only operating in Perspective Theory on the gains side: it is, as it were, a pseudo-wealth effect. The substitution effect brought into play by the increased benefits at the margin to be derived from holding an extra unit of wealth in asset one rather than in asset two, which will work in favour of asset one, is counteracted by the implicit wealth effect on the gain side that is induced by the fact that the average increase in gain for given loss is also increased. It is not necessary even

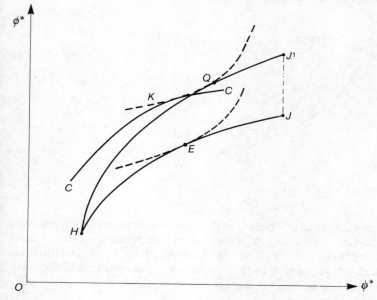

*Figure 4.7*

to maintain the previous holding of asset one. If that negative pseudo-wealth effect is sufficiently strong it could cause the same or even a reduced value of asset one in the portfolio.

The $\phi^\star = f(\psi^\star)$, optimum trade-off function over gain and loss ascendancy indices, for the case of just two risky assets will be shifted from $HJ$ to $HJ'$ in Figure 4.7. The point $H$ will represent the combination of $\phi^\star$ and $\psi^\star$ which can be attained when all of the investor's wealth is placed into asset two. Similarly, point $J$ denotes the $\phi^\star$ and $\psi^\star$ for the total investment of wealth in asset one, the 'riskier' asset. Only $\beta_1$ has changed, therefore $J'$ must lie immediately above $J$: only at $H$ can the new trade-off frontier coincide with the original.

Let us assume that the initial optimum position selected was at $E$ and that the new one is located at $Q$ on $HJ'$. The curve $CC$ is parallel to the original frontier and is tangential to the new optimum $P$-indifference curve at $K$. The move from $E$ to $K$ can be used to represent the pseudo-wealth effect, and that from $K$ to $Q$ can represent the pure substitution effect of a reduction in $\beta_1$. The latter effect works in favour of an increase in $x_1$; hence in favour of an increase in both $\phi^\star$ and $\psi^\star$. I have assumed that the wealth effect embodied in the perspective function leads to a reduction in $\psi^\star$

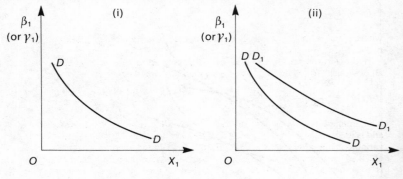

*Figure 4.8*

but an increase in $\phi^\star$ (hence, in this two-asset case under my working hypotheses, has led to a reduction in the holding of $x_1$). I have assumed that the net effect, as determined by $P$, its constituents, $\phi^\star$ and $\psi^\star$, is positive in that $\psi^\star$ increases; consequently, the own-response *ceteris paribus* impact of an improvement in the gain-potential of asset one is positive.

If $\gamma_1$ is reduced, *ceteris paribus*, the consequences for portfolio composition noted above will apply *mutatis mutandis*. The same is true should there be *ceteris paribus* adjustments to either $\beta_2$ or $\gamma_2$.

My particular specification of the Perspective Theory asset selection model produces definitive effects on portfolio composition when only the investor's wealth level changes. On the supposition that any such alteration is not of sufficient magnitude to influence $\psi(.)$ or $P(.)$, increases in wealth will be allocated in the same proportion across all the assets originally held in the portfolio. All asset demand equations are multiplicative in wealth.

The demand equation for any asset can be depicted in the traditional fashion as the *ceteris paribus* function of its own price-equivalent characteristics, shifting, or strengthening, as wealth increases. Figure 4.8 illustrates those functions for the Perspective Theory model of portfolio choice.

The demand equation in my specific version of the model can be convex or concave to the origin since, as equation (4.52) reveals, without extra hypotheses, the second derivative of $\partial(x_1/W)\partial\beta_1$ has an indeterminate sign. In Figure 4.8, the curve $D_1D_1$ represents a doubling of $W$ from its original level along $DD$.

*Notes*

1  Suppose then that the probability distribution of returns on some one asset, $r$, were to possess this normal probability density function:

$$f(r) = \frac{e^{-\frac{1}{2}(\frac{r-\mu}{\sigma})^2}}{\sigma\sqrt{2\pi}}$$

(i)

where $\mu$ and $\sigma$ denote as always the mean and the variance of the random variable, $r$.

If the returns on $r$ are scaled up by assuming that as one possible portfolio all of wealth, $W$, could be held in asset one, it is discovered that:

$$f(rW) = \frac{1}{(\sigma W)\sqrt{2\pi}} \int_{-\infty}^{\infty} e^{-\frac{1}{2}(\frac{rW - W\mu}{W\sigma})^2}$$

(ii)

The integral is $(\sigma W)\sqrt{2\pi}$ (the proof by change of variable is straightforward and is identical with the textbook proof that the integral of any normally distributed variable is one): hence $f(rW)$ is a normally distributed random variable with mean of $(W\mu)$ and variance of $(W\sigma)^2$; as required if the probability density function is to apply to scaled up values of individual asset returns. In general, where a combination of assets is being selected, the holding of asset $i$, $x_i$, will be less than wealth. However, $r_i x_i = R_i$ will be normally distributed. So too will $R_j$ if $r_j$ is normally distributed. Then both $R_i$ and $R_j$ will possess moment generating functions of this kind:

$$M_R(t) = e^{\mu t + \frac{1}{2}\sigma^2 t^2}.$$

If it is supposed that $R_i$ and $R_j$ are independent, then the moment generating function for $(R_i + R_j)$ will be that of a normally distributed random variable since $M_{R_i + R_j}(t)$ is the product of $M_{R_i}(t)$ and $M_{R_j}(t)$. The distribution $f(R_i + R_j) = f(r_i x_i + r_j x_j)$ will have mean equal to $\mu_i x_i + \mu_j x_j$ and a variance $\sigma_i^2 x_i^2 + \sigma_j^2 x_j^2$.

2 Apart from the fact that the available range of discrete distributions is limited, most do not permit any appropriate scaling of the returns on individual assets. Their main deficiency is that, *ex definitione*, they do not permit asset holdings to be in anything other than integer values.

3 Since $f(R) = F'(R)$.

4 This is from equations (4.34) and (4.35) with $\alpha_i = \gamma_i = 2$ and from equation (4.33).

5 This result is derived from the standard formula for block inversion of a partitioned matrix. If we let:

$$Q = \begin{bmatrix} z_1 B - z_2 T & \vdots & i \\ \cdots & \cdots & \cdots \\ i' & \vdots & 0 \end{bmatrix} = \begin{bmatrix} A & \vdots & Z \\ \cdots & \cdots & \cdots \\ C & \vdots & D \end{bmatrix};$$

where: $A$ is $n \times n$; $Z$ is $n \times 1$; $C$ is $1 \times n$; $D$ is $1 \times 1$, we can write:

$$Q^{-1} = \begin{bmatrix} A^{-1}(I + ZE^{-1}CA^{-1}) & -A^{-1}ZE^{-1} \\ -E^{-1}CA^{-1} & E^{-1} \end{bmatrix};$$

provided that: $|A| \neq 0$ and $|E| \neq 0$, where: $E = D - CA^{-1}Z$.

6 They sum to: $D\left(\frac{2z_1}{\beta_1^2} - \frac{2z_1}{\beta_1^2 \beta_2}\right) + \frac{\partial D}{\partial \beta_1}[a_{22} + a_{11} - 2a_{12}].$

The expression in square brackets is simply $-D$, therefore the sum is zero because $\partial D/\partial \beta_1$ equals the term in round brackets.

# 5 Choice Under Uncertainty: Some Wider Applications of Perspective Theory

There are, to state a platitude, numerous situations in which individual and corporate decision-makers have to select just one course of action or strategy to pursue out of many, when their knowledge of the outcomes of their actions is almost unknown; at best they are bounded by historical or conventional limits. Very few choices are made in a fixed-odds, gambler/lottery ticket, environment.

Again, many of the contexts in which decisions are taken will not be of purely, or perhaps even partial, economic nature. I would doubt if any model of human behaviour under uncertainty is capable of embracing all possible decisions that have to be effected under some degree of unknowledge. Yet, even in the confines of economic decision-making it seems to be too ambitious to hope that one kind of decision framework will suit all purposes: even within a subject area the appropriate model seems likely to be context dependent. The context can be defined in terms of several factors, for example: the state of knowledge of the decision-maker about the consequences of his action-choices, which would embrace the possibility that he might be faced with objective odds; the speed with which the decision has to be taken; the constraints on the individual's choices, such as fixed commitments, which may not be of an economic nature, which limit his degree of manoeuvrability so he 'plays for safety'; and the knowledge available for solving the decision problems. These points have already been noted in Part I and especially the view of Heiner (1983) that the last mentioned, concerned as it is with the skills and knowledge of the decision-makers themselves, is the paramount restriction on the type of decision-making framework that can be, or indeed is, utilized by them.

The numerous decision-making situations that have to be assimilated by individual agents should not be expected *a priori* to be explicable by reference to one paradigm. Even for a given action-choice problem the models or, in less grandiose language, the processes used by decision-making units can differ; probably, largely through Heiner's 'individual capacity effect'.

This has been recognized in the, now voluminous, literature that exists on the 'microeconomics of uncertainty'. That literature has devoted itself to consideration of issues of this kind (in addition to portfolio selection) in a world of uncertainty (or rather risk, as it happens): the choice of real capital investment; the optimal work–leisure choice, when income is uncertain; the optimum consumption–saving pattern, when the return on saving is uncertain; the optimal degree of search, for employment and for consumption goods when, respectively, the going wage and the going price are not known beforehand; and price or output levels, as appropriate, if the business man is unsure about the demand for, or the price of, his product.

This list is meant only to be illustrative. It could be extended considerably, although it does provide a reasonable indication of the categories of issues that have so far been tackled in the literature. Apart from my own attempt to apply Shackle's Theory and the Fordian (Shacklesque) model to these kinds of problems (*see* Ford 1983), the whole of the existing literature has used either the Expected Utility Theory or variants of it, either through mean/variance analysis or its Safety-First version. In fact, the Safety-First models have been employed only for the investigation of portfolio choice (*see*, for example, Roy 1952; Pyle and Turnovsky 1970; and Ford 1983) and for analysing the behaviour of the firm under uncertainty (*see*, for example, Arzac 1976). The predominant model, however, has been that of Expected Utility Theory. Indeed, that theory has been applied to decision-making in all of the above areas and, where it has had its major impact, to the question of portfolio selection.

Some of the decision choices listed above will now be considered in the light of Perspective Theory. As some of the probabilistically based literature has recognized in advocating the use of Safety-First paradigms instead of the Expected Utility Theory, we shall recognize that Perspective Theory as outlined so far might itself require a change of perspective to enable it to give an intuitively appealing view of action-choice. However, it is advisable to retain the essential spirit of the framework developed previously, which was focused on choice over lotteries and portfolios, which are effectively lotteries, but potentially over gains and losses.

## A Two-Period Consumption–Saving Model

There are many variants and developments of consumption–saving choice in a world of uncertainty, which are prevalent in the orthodox literature. However, the basic model of such choice, which first extended the textbook, certain world, Fisherian version of this action-choice, will be sufficient for my purposes (Sandmo 1970).

A consumer, or household-unit, is envisaged to have a utility function $U(.)$ over his consumption in periods one and two only, namely $C_1$ and $C_2$. To put some reality into this framework, we might, as the literature has since tended to do, think of these as the period of working life and the period of retirement. The consumer is alleged to know his earned income in periods one and two, labelled $Y_1$ and $Y_2$, respectively. Now, his consumption in period one will be determined by his income in period one, there being no yield he can receive as a supplement to his earned income, from the yield on previous savings, *ex hypothesi*. In period two he is assumed to spend all of the income that he receives. That income can differ from his earned income by the yield on any saving he has undertaken in period one. The consumer is alleged to spend all of the income he does receive in period two. That income must equal $Y_2 + (Y_1 - C_1)r$; where $Y_1 - C_1$ is saving in period one, namely $S_1$, and $r$ is the yield on a unit value of saving, invested perhaps in bonds.

The uncertainty variant of this Fisherian story appears via the hypothesis that $r$ is unknown. In the conventional literature it is supposed to possess a known probability density function, $f(r)$. The choice, indeed, that the consumer now has to make, so it is postulated is to select that value of $C_1$ (hence of $S_1$) which will maximize the expected value of utility, utility having become stochastic because of the random nature of $r$.

Hence, the formal problem is:

$$\max_{C_1} E(U) = \int_a^b U(C_1, (Y_1 - C_1)r)f(r)dr \qquad (5.1$$

Here I have made the substitution that $C_2 \equiv (Y_1 - C_1)r$ *ex hypothesi* and $(a,b)$ denote the (known) limits over which $r$ will fluctuate.

How could Perspective Theory analyse the choice of current consumption in these conditions? In principle, I would suggest that the framework laid down – I might even be bold enough to say established – in the preceding chapters will be applicable *per se*. The *modus operandi* of the consumer will be to select that level of $C_1$ which promises him the best combination of $\phi^\star$ and $\psi^\star$, because it may be assumed that, even if $f(r)$ were known, in essence, that a probabilistic approach was possible, it will indicate that $r$ is spread across gains and losses, if $r$ relates to a true financial asset. That yield will encompass positive and negative movements in the price of the 'bonds', which in the case of price reduction could countervail the pure interest effect.

Note here that $C_2$ depends upon the definite $Y_2$ and the variable unknown $(Y_1 - C_1)r$, and, essentially, the latter should be envisaged as the value of savings when period two is reached.[1] The figure $(Y_1 - C_1)r$ *per se* can never be negative: but, crucially, the value of $S_I$ can increase or decrease over the unit investment period. In short, the value of what I would regard here as the investor's level of investable wealth, $S_I$, can rise or fall as a consequence of the fluctuations in $r$.

By the end of the investment period the consumer will have received a pure interest payment (if the bond carries a coupon payment), which must equal $S_I$ times $R$, the pure rate of interest. In addition he will have a cash surrender value of his savings equal to $S_I B_P$, where $B_P$ is the ratio of the price of a bond at the outset of period two over that at the start of period one. Therefore, investment income, $I$, is defined as:[2]

$$I = (Y_I - C_I)[R_I + B_P]$$ (5.2)

$$\therefore I = (Y_I - C_I)\left[R_I + \frac{R_I}{R_2}\right]$$ (5.3)

The uncertain part of the yield on saving, of course, arises because of the possible change in the ratio of $R_I/R_2$, the pure rate of interest. If $R_2$ rises above $R_I$, the rate of interest at the date the investment was transacted, then the value of wealth falls over the investment period. The probability density function applies to $R_2$.

If it is supposed that $f(R_2)$ is known to the investor it could be used to depict the increase and reduction in wealth that could occur: the resulting distributions would differ as initial $S_I$ or wealth alters, just as the gain/loss distribution does in the portfolio selection model where the choice is not the level of wealth to invest, but how much to allocate to competing assets.[3] Taking into account for each $S_I$ the certain yield it provides, as $S_I$ changes a series of probability density and cumulative distribution functions over $C_2$ can be deduced. The consumer then chooses the level of $C_2$ which maximizes $P = f(\phi^\star, \psi^\star)$. We can think of $P(.)$ exactly as we have done previously, but since the $\phi^\star$ of current consumption is affected by the choice of $C_2$ (whilst, by construction, $\psi^\star(C_2) = 0$) we have to amend $\phi$ so that it depends upon $\phi_I$ and $\phi_2$, which could be in an additive or multiplicative fashion; reflecting time preference if we so wish by the consumer's attaching more weight to $\phi_I$.

The analysis in that case for the probabilistic version of Perspective Theory, based on continuous probability density functions, is complex. With discrete distributions, especially of an arbitrary limited state of nature form which is more apposite than the textbook distributions (such as, say, the Poisson, limited as they are to integer values and values defined sometimes up to $\infty$ ), the analysis is readily accomplished. However, we can, in essence, only describe and portray how the choice of $C_I$ is reached. Without postulating some kind of continuous function for the returns on saving, it is not possible to derive 'general' results.

One possible avenue (which I have pursued) is to postulate that the consumer can invest only in irredeemable government bonds which promise a zero coupon payment. The consumer's preoccupation is then with the future: to present price ratio of bonds ($B_P$). Assuming that that ratio possesses a normal distribution with a mean of unity, it will promise a 50 per cent chance of the value of wealth declining and likewise a 50 per cent chance that it will increase. The consumer is then faced by distributions of the end-of-period wealth $(Y_1 - C_1)B_P$ that will have different variances depending upon the scalar variable $(Y_1 - C_1)$. He then chooses that level of $C_1$ which maximizes, say:

$$P = \alpha\phi^\star - \beta\psi^\star; \alpha \neq \beta \tag{5.4}$$

with, say:

$$\phi = \phi_1 + \phi_2 \tag{5.5}$$
$$\psi = \psi_1 + \psi_2 \tag{5.6}$$

and, furthermore, for example:

$$\phi_1 = \phi_1(C_1, 1), \phi_2 = \phi_2(Y_2 + (Y_1 - C_1)B_P, \Pi_{C2});$$

with $\Pi_{C2}$ denoting the probability attached to $C_2$, in effect, to $B_P$. Of course, positive time-preference rather than neutral time-preference could be assumed for $\phi(.)$.

In applying the $\theta$-function version of Perspective Theory to the consumer's consumption-saving problem let it be assumed as an initial example that the asset in which the consumer can invest his saving is an irredeemable government bond with a zero coupon. This means that the consumer has to form some expectations in his mind concerning the likely movements upwards and downwards of the price of bonds. His $\theta$-functions are unlikely to be continuous on either side of the value of one, the no-change situation for bond prices; and depending upon recent trends in asset prices it is more than likely that he will have a few values that he thinks the price of bonds will assume for only one period, clustered around the ratio of unity. The recent trend might very well just become an upward one; in which case, given his views about government monetary and fiscal policy, it is possible that the spread of ratios of the future to the present bond price will be 'skewed' to the right of unity.

Nevertheless, to provide a formal, mathematical treatment of the applications of Perspective Theory to the current choice problem, I shall assume that the $\theta$-function over gains and losses of value in wealth (that is, of current saving) are continuous up to certain

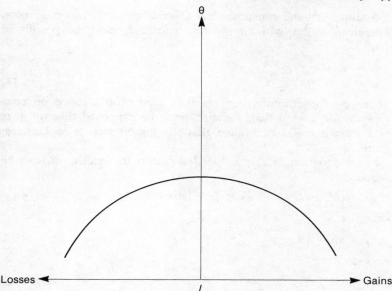

*Figure 5.1*

limits. I shall also hypothesize that they are the mirror image of
one another to expedite the analysis. So, let the θ-function be as
depicted in Figure 5.1.

Formally:

$$\lambda = a - b\theta_G - c\theta_G^2; \lambda > 1 \tag{5.7}$$
$$\mu = a - b\theta_L - c\theta_L^2; \mu < 1 \tag{5.8}$$

In equation (5.7) $\lambda$ is for the ratio of the bond price in period
two to that in period one, when the ratio exceeds one; to avoid
confusion over symbols, $\mu$ replaces $\lambda$ for the case where the ratio
is below unity.

The parabolic form for the θ-function enables us to operate with
a mathematically more tractable function for $\phi$ than I have been
using to encapsulate the balancing of outcome against likelihood
or degree of credibility. It can be assumed that $\phi(.)$ and $\psi(.)$ take
on a linear form. Thus let:

$$\phi = n\theta_G + tG; n,t > 0 \tag{5.9}$$
$$\psi = n\theta_L + tL \tag{5.10}$$

$G$ and $L$ are the gains and losses in wealth above and below the
initial wealth of $(Y_1 - C_1)$; $G$ being equal to $(Y_1 - C_1)\lambda$.

Assume that the consumer has neutral time-preference for now. Therefore it can, without too much loss of detail, be postulated that:

$$\phi = \phi_1 + \phi_2 \tag{5.11}$$
$$\psi = \psi_1 + \psi_2 \tag{5.12}$$

where $\phi_1$, for example, denotes the value of $\phi(.)$ based on consumption in period two. Further, let it be supposed that $\psi_1 = 0$; in a way, it could be argued that the logical step is to make $\psi_1 = \min \phi_1$.

From equation (5.7) the 'portfolio' gain in wealth, $y_G$, can be deduced.

$$y_G = (Y_1 - C_1)\lambda - x\lambda = [a - b\theta_G - c\theta_G^2]x \tag{5.13}$$

Likewise:

$$y_L = x\mu = [a - b\theta_L - c\theta_L^2]x \tag{5.14}$$

*Ex hypothesi:*

$$\phi_1 = n\theta_{max} + t(C_1) \tag{5.15}$$

The consumer must locate the value of $\theta_G$ that, for given $C_1$, will maximize the value of $\phi_2(.)$; and likewise for $\theta_L$.

Thus, from equations (5.9) and (5.13):

$$\theta_G = \frac{n - bt(x)}{2ct(x)}; \lambda > 1 \tag{5.16}$$

$$\theta_L = \frac{n - bt(x)}{2ct(x)}; \mu < 1 \tag{5.17}$$

From equation (5.17) utilizing $\theta_G$ given by equation (5.16) we discover the value of $y_G$ which maximizes $\phi(.)$ for a pre-assigned value of $C_1$, given the constraint on $\phi$ imposed by equation (5.13) itself:

$$y_G = ax - bc\left[\frac{n - bt(x)}{2ct(x)}\right] - cx\left[\frac{n - bt(x)}{2ct(x)}\right]^2 \tag{5.18}$$

This permits us to write out $\phi = \phi_1 + \phi_2$ since $\phi_2 = n\theta_G + t(Y_2 + y_G)$; with $\theta_G$ and $y_G$ at their optimum, $\theta_G^*$ and $y_G^*$ levels epitomized in equations (5.16) and (5.17). Following an identical process $\psi_2$ can be specified in full.

Assume that:

$$P = \alpha\phi - \beta\psi = \alpha(\phi_1 + \phi_2) - \beta\psi_2 \tag{5.19}$$

Then, from my assumptions the value of $C_1$ that will maximize the perspective index is to be unscrambled from:

$$\alpha \frac{d\phi_1}{dC_1} + (\alpha - \beta) \frac{d\phi_2}{dC_1} = 0 \tag{5.20}$$

Therefore:

$$\alpha t + (\beta - \alpha)\left[ \frac{n^2}{4ctx^2} - at - \frac{bn}{2cx^2} - \frac{bt}{4c} \right] = 0$$

$$\therefore x^2 = \frac{(\beta - \alpha)[2bnt - n^2]}{4ct[\alpha t + t(\alpha - \beta)(a + \frac{b}{4c})]} \tag{5.21}$$

from which $C_1$ can be extracted from the definition of $x$ as $Y_1 - C_1$, letting the right hand side of (5.21) be $\Delta$:

$$C_1^2 - 2C_1 Y = \Delta - Y_1^2 \tag{5.22}$$

As in Expected Utility Theory, the demand for current consumption depends upon the behavioural attitudes of the consumer, and upon the promises of increases and reductions in wealth that are possible. The reduction in $C_1$ will promise a higher value of $G$ at any given $\theta$; and so a pull will be exerted on the consumer's mind. Nevertheless that can be halted from the push that is generated on the loss side: the increased saving will bring with it the possibility of higher reductions in wealth value. The consumer has to balance those competing prospects as they gain ascendancy in his mind: and he has to do so against the fact that increasing saving, whilst, perhaps, promising some positive value of the scanning, perspective index can do so only by causing a certain reduction in current consumption, and hence, *ceteris paribus*, in his $\phi$ and $P$ indices. The presence of positive-time preference would serve to increase the level of current consumption, all other behavioural parameters remaining unchanged.

How, given the assumed behaviour pattern of the consumer, would he react to changes in his own expectations about the yield on saving? The analogous question in Expected Utility Theory concerns itself with the responsiveness of current consumption to an alteration in the mean value or in the variance of the yield distribution. It brings forth the conventional, ambiguous answer, that if, say, the mean value of the yield increases, the consumer might or might not decide to consume less now and take on the chance of a higher, even though risky, future level of consumption. The precise answer depends upon the strength of the familiar wealth and substitution effects. In the $\theta$-function portrayal of Perspective Theory (and in its probability format) the answer is essentially the same.

When the consumer is more sanguine about the returns on saving, he will reduce $b$ or $c$ or both in $\theta_G(.)$; and/or he will increase $b$ or $c$ or both in $\theta_L(.)$. On my simplifying assumptions I have marked the influence of a change in only one side of the overall $\theta(.)$ by assuming that $\theta_G(.) = \theta_L(.)$. However, it is still possible to see the effect of a change in expectations. Suppose that $b$ is reduced; this raises $\phi^*$ at any given level of $C_1$; it also increases $\psi^*$. To attain any level of $\phi^*$ it is now not necessary to retain the level of $C_1$; reducing it allows for the potential to reduce $\psi^*$ despite the unfavourable shift in $\theta_L(.)$. Here is the 'wealth' effect at work; the pure substitution effect would induce the consumer (given the properties I have assumed for the perspective function) to choose less of $C_1$.

Suppose there is a *ceteris paribus* reduction in $c$:

$$\text{sign } \frac{dC_1}{dc} = \text{sign } \frac{\Delta(\alpha + (\alpha - \beta)a)4}{4\alpha c + 4(\alpha - \beta)ac + (\alpha - \beta)b} \qquad (5.23)$$

In view of the restriction that $C_1 \leqslant Y_1$, inspection of equation (5.22) permits us to deduce that $\Delta > 0$ for $C_1 > 0$. The sign of $dC_1/dc$ rests upon the sign of $\alpha - \beta$. If the latter is positive, $C_1$ and $c$ must be related positively: a reduction in $c$ will lead to a reduction in $C_1$ and hence to an increase in $C_2 = S_1$, given initial wealth. The substitution effect has dominated the 'wealth' effect; with $\phi^*$ valued more highly than $\psi^*$. The increase in $\phi^*$ is given more (positive) weight than the weight (negative) assigned to the ineluctable increase in $\psi^*$.

Is it possible to say what will happen, *ceteris paribus*, if there should be an increase in $Y_1$? Again, this is a standard question in the Expected Utility version of this form of paradigm. The answer is immediate: all of the increase in current earned income will be consumed in the current period. From equation (5.17), $dY_1 \equiv dC_1$.

This is not the outcome if $P(.)$ is altered to the effect that the term in $\psi^*$ becomes $-\beta(\psi^*)^2$. In that event, both $C_1$ and $C_2$ can increase, as might be expected *a priori*. Additionally the level of future earned income, $Y_2$, influences the level of current consumption and saving. As $Y_2$ increases, the effect on $C_1$ is indeterminate depending upon the usual 'wealth' and substitution effects.

## A Labour Choice Model

This matter has also been discussed extensively in the Expected Utility literature. I shall take one of the simplest models, that utilized by Block and Heineke (1973). The model is a one-period model. The individual, or the household, is assumed to be faced with a decision as to what quantity of labour ($N$) to supply given that earned income ($wN$) is stochastic because $w$, the wage rate, is random. The individual is supposed to possess a utility function $U(.)$ of this form:

$$U = U(N, wN) \qquad (5.24)$$

The hypothesis is that there is a known probability density function for $w$, $f(w)$. Accordingly, it is assumed that in order to act rationally in the face of that 'uncertainty', the individual should decide upon the best value of $N$ by maximizing the expected value of $U(.)$.

These genre of models are all rather contrived, but suppose that the individual was concerned to solve this problem period-by-period. If the distribution of $w$ is not known, and if search is excluded as it is in this framework, by construction – because the implication is that the labourer will know the definite wage once he has agreed to work for an employer (but that he has to contract beforehand for the amount of labour he will offer $(N)$) – then he has only his anticipations or hunches to guide him as to whether it is worth offering $x$ amount of labour services and sacrificing the residual leisure time. Will the compensations for the disutility of work be high enough?

Confronted by this game against the employer, or against nature if 'the' market decides what the actual wage will be, the individual will map out his likely expectation of the wage rate. He will select the range in which he anticipates that the wage must lie and then he will assign to each wage that seems feasible to him within that range a degree of credibility. It cannot possibly be stated what his $\theta$-function will look like. However suppose, for illustrative purposes, that it assumes the form depicted in Figure 5.2.

The range of $w$ is $ab$. As $N$ varies total income, $wN$, naturally, will possess a different $\theta$-function. Each $\theta$-function for $wN$ will be $\theta(w)$ scaled up by $N$, just as portfolio returns were simple scaled-up values of returns on individual assets. It is self-evident that the larger is $N$, the higher is $wN$ at any $\theta$: the lowest and the highest values of $\phi$ will be associated with the highest value of $N$.

There are no possibilities of losses to sharpen the focus of the labourer. The level of $N$ does not only condition $wN$, and, therefore, the values of $\phi_{max}$ and $\phi_{min}$. It is also likely to impinge on the investor's utility or satisfaction directly, as in equation (5.24) and as conventional labour supply literature under certainty has assumed.

How can an approach such as that offered by Perspective Theory be used? I would suggest that the way forward is immediate. The individual can be assumed to be seeking to choose $N$ to maximize equation (5.24) under certainty, and its counterpart under uncertainty would be:

$$\phi = \phi(N, wN, \theta_{wN}) \qquad (5.25)$$

The ascendancy of any choice of $N$ depends upon the $N$ itself,

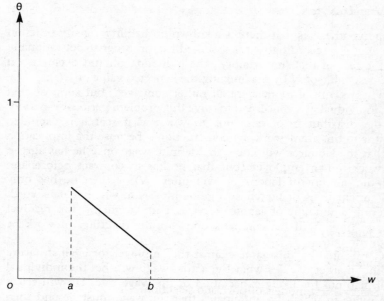

*Figure 5.2*

the anticipated income it will bring, and the degree of credibility attached to the occurrence of that receipt. It might be expected *a priori* that the sign of the partial derivatives of $\phi$ would be:

$$\phi_N < 0; \; \phi_{wN} > 0; \; \phi_\theta > 0.$$

The fact that increasing $N$ will produce higher values of $\phi$ via $wN$ and $\theta$ (on the basis of the $w(\theta)$ drawn in Figure 5.2) will be countervailed by the negative effect on $\phi$ that is imparted through the higher value of $N$. The choice of $N$ is not necessarily a trivial one.

With no losses possible the paradigm that I have advocated for investment/lottery choice, and in the preceding section for decisions under uncertainty that have investment outcomes implicitly as their element of uncertainty, needs modification. I have already emphasized that it is asking too much of any theoretical construct that it have universal application. Once we move away from investment choices, or those involving losses or danger level outcomes, we may need to look for modifications of the basic structure that make it amenable to handling the relevant choice of action.

One obvious avenue to suggest and explore is that $\psi^\star_{max}$ be replaced by $\phi_{min}$. That can be accommodated in this example; it retains the 'best', 'worst', ascendancy trade-off that seems to be the best way of characterizing, maybe parodying, choice under uncertainty. Only one outcome can occur; a perspective has to be taken of the range of alternatives, the general feel of a set of prospects has to be captured in some measure; but the Safety-First net provided by also keeping uppermost in the mind the worst that the prospect could offer seems the way to telescope the expectational prospects that are promised. To give them all weight when one alone will count once the choice of action has been made seems incongruous.

The concept of a safety net can, alternatively, be captured analytically by advocating the view that the individual decision-maker will have in mind a minimum value of $\phi$ below which he will not offer his labour. This represents a reservation value of $\phi$, as it were. In reality this would perhaps be the $\phi$ generated by an income equal to the level of unemployment benefit. This can be conceived of as a pseudo-aspiration level of the Henry Simon kind mentioned in Chapters 1 and 3.

In some analyses, of course, the reservation parameter, whatever it might be – wage rate, price of goods under search – is an endogenous variable. Here I am proposing that it is exogenous, as in Safety-First models of portfolio selection.

To effect variety, let it be assumed that the labourer in my current model has a reservation value of $\phi$; call this $\phi_D$. If the best $\phi$ that he can obtain with his labour services, whatever that $N$ might be, is below $\phi_{min}$, then he accepts 'leisure' and goes on the dole, or he dis-saves.

The choice of $N$, naturally, becomes that $N$ which provides the largest $\phi - \phi_D$. In principle, this amounts to our searching for the $N$ that maximizes $\phi$, as $\phi_D$ can be thought as normalized at zero. The perspective index adjusted so that it is $P = f(\phi - \phi_D)$ has become $P = \phi$.

In the model specifically formalized above it can be deduced that, by choosing $N$ to maximize the part of $\phi(.)$ dependent upon ($wN$, $\theta$) for a pre-determined value of N, the maximum maximiorium level of $\phi^\star$ is to be selected on the following basis:

$$\phi^\star = \delta N + \alpha\left[a_oN - a_1N\left(\frac{2\alpha Na_o - \beta}{2\alpha a_1^2 N}\right)\right]^2 + \beta\left(\frac{2\alpha Na_o - \beta}{2\alpha a_1^2 N}\right) \tag{5.26}$$

To derive this equation based on the $\phi^\star = f(N)$, I have used these assumptions:

$$w = a_o - a_1\theta \tag{5.27}$$

$$\phi = \delta N + \alpha(wN)^2 + \beta\theta \tag{5.28}$$

The individual's optimum quantity of labour services, $N$, is derived from differentiation of equation (5.26):

$$\left[ \delta + \frac{\beta a_0}{a_1}(1 - \frac{1}{a_1}) \right] N + 2\alpha a_0^2 (1 - \frac{1}{a_1})(1 - \frac{1}{a_1^2})N^2 + \frac{\beta^2}{2\alpha a_1^2} = 0 \tag{5.29}$$

Should $a_1$ be normalized at unity, the analytic solution equation for $N$ is reduced to a first-degree polynomial:

$$N = \frac{-\beta^2}{2\alpha\delta} > 0; \delta < 0 \tag{5.30}$$

To investigate the effect of a change in $w(\theta)$, the expectations of the wage rate, we need to retain equation (5.29) in full. If $a_1 \neq 1$, an increase in $a_0$, which means that the household unit has become more optimistic about the wage to be offered, could lead to an increase, decrease or no change, in the quantity of labour services supplied:

$$\frac{\partial N}{\partial a_0} = \frac{\frac{\beta}{a_1}(\frac{1}{a_1} - 1)N + 4\alpha a_0(\frac{1}{a_1} - 1)(1 - \frac{1}{a_1^2})N^2}{\delta + \frac{\beta a_0}{a_1}(1 - \frac{1}{a_1}) + 4\alpha a_0^2(1 - \frac{1}{a_1})(1 - \frac{1}{a_1^2})N} \tag{5.31}$$

An increase in $a_0$, an unequivocal improvement in the wage prospects, will not necessarily lead to an increase in $N$. The 'income effect' is pulling against the substitution effect generated by the shift in $w(\theta)$. The net effect depends, as in orthodox theory, upon the properties of the expectational function, $w(\theta)$, and of the preference ordering, balancing 'goods' against 'bads', in the form of $(\alpha, \beta)$ and $(\delta)$ respectively.

## Output Choice under Price Uncertainty for the Perfectly Competitive Firm

This too is an issue that has been addressed in much of the literature in recent years. The main vehicle used for tackling it has been the Expected Utility model; though there has been a movement towards adopting the Safety-First version of the probabilistic paradigm (*see*, for example, Arzac 1976). Here I rely upon the simple, seminal framework, utilized by Sandmo (1971), based as it was on the Expected Utility Theory.

An entrepreneur produces and sells his product, $x_1$, in a competitive market. The price of the product, $P$, is not known before he has to select the level of output, $Q$, that he is to produce and sell (the model is a textbook static one, so there are no inventories). His fixed costs are known (FC); the only variable costs he incurs

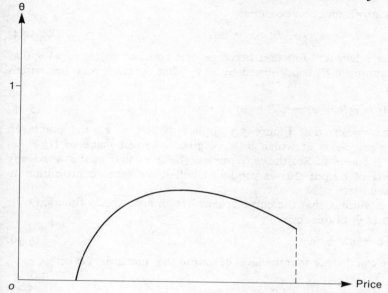

*Figure 5.3*

are attributable to the hiring of labour ($N$), those costs being equal simply to the wage rate ($w$) times $N$. It is postulated that $w$ is known to the entrepreneur when he has to choose $Q$. The probability density function for $P$ is known, $f(P)$.

The entrepreneur is assumed to possess a utility function over profit ($\lambda$), namely $U = U(\lambda)$. Since $P$ is stochastic, so too is $\lambda$. The entrepreneur, it is argued, selects $Q$ by maximizing the expected value of $U(.)$. The labour requirements of the firm are assumed dependent upon the level of output given the fixed stock of capital and the state of technology.

The profit level is given by:

$$\lambda = PQ - wN - FC \qquad (5.32)$$

with $N = f(Q)$ as the short-run production function. The only unknown is $P$: assume that the entrepreneur's $\theta$-function for $P$ happens to be a continuous one and can be depicted by Figure 5.3.

Since $w$ is known, if it should happen that the short-run production function exhibits only weak diminishing returns to labour at the margin, so that $N = f(Q)$ can be approximated by a linear function:

$$N = qQ \qquad (5.33)$$

the profit function becomes:

$$\lambda = (P - z)Q - FC; z = wq \qquad (5.34)$$

The relevant $\theta$-function becomes that attached to $(P - z)$ – that is simply $\theta(P)$ transformed by $- z$. That function may be written as:

$$\theta = b(P - z) + c(P - z)^2; c < 0 \qquad (5.35)$$

This means that Figure 5.3 applies to $\theta(P - z)$, the points on the price-axis at which $\theta = 0$, gives a lowest value of $(P - z)$ of $-b/c > 0$. So, the entrepreneur believes that at the worst any level of output that is produced will make some contribution to fixed costs.

Assuming that the entrepreneur has an ascendancy function over $\lambda$ and $\theta_\lambda$ of this form:

$$\phi = \alpha\lambda + \beta\theta_\lambda \qquad (5.36)$$

we can deduce that the level of output that maximizes $\phi$ is:

$$Q = \frac{2\alpha + \beta b}{\alpha} = Q^\star \qquad (5.37)$$

The worst value of $\phi$ that could occur for any $Q$ depends upon the lowest value of $(P - z)$. Under the assumptions I have made that value is independent of $Q$ (in effect because it is independent of $N$ via $N = f(Q)$). Therefore $Q^\star$ produces the highest and lowest values of $\phi : \phi_{min} \simeq \psi_{max}$ can be ignored. The entrepreneur knows that for any $Q$ the worst outcome that he anticipates according to his $\theta$-function for the price of his product is not a disaster. The minimum keeps him afloat.

It can be seen, indeed, that in the above presentation the level of *FC* does not influence the choice of output. In the theory of the firm under certainty an increase in fixed costs must leave the output of the firm unaffected; it merely serves to reduce the level of profit. In the Expected Utility version of this model an increase in fixed costs will lower output. If the entrepreneur is a risk-averter and his mathematical expectation of the price of his product equals the market price that would have ruled under certainty, his output will be lower than what he would have produced under certainty.

I shall therefore adjust my preceding specification to inquire about the possible effects on output of an alteration in fixed costs, because, on the behavioural and technological assumptions I have assumed to condition the entrepreneur's choice of output level, they become otiose. The second issue also has little substance in the light of the previous model.

The model could, therefore, be amended in two ways. The first is by assuming that:

$$N = \mu Q + \delta Q^2 \; ; \mu, \delta > 0 \qquad (5.38)$$

and the second is by postulating:

$$\phi = \alpha\lambda^2 + \beta\theta_L \qquad (5.39)$$

The first assumption makes the choice of output less obvious than previously: the aim of maximizing $Q$, which in effect became the objective, is no longer valid, because increasing $Q$ increases $N$ and hence $wN$, so reducing anticipated profit.

To use either or both of (5.38) and (5.39) and produce 'general' findings, $\theta(P)$ needs simplifying. Suppose:

$$\theta = a - bP \qquad (5.40)$$

Utilizing both (5.38) and (5.39) leads to a sixth-degree polynomial in the optimum level of output: a level that depends upon the parameters of $N = f(Q)$, $\theta(P)$ and of $\phi(.)$, and upon Fixed Costs.[4] Assume, therefore, that either (5.38) or (5.39) obtains.

Consider the former first of all: to enrich the findings, however, $\phi(.)$ is adjusted so that (5.39) is replaced by:

$$\phi = \alpha\lambda + \beta(\theta_\lambda)^2 \qquad (5.41)$$

$\lambda$ becomes:

$$\lambda = \left[\frac{a - \theta}{b}\right] Q - w\mu Q - w\delta Q^2 - FC \qquad (5.42)$$

Taken in conjunction with (5.41), the value of $\theta$, for given $Q$, that maximizes $\phi$ is:

$$\theta^\star = \frac{Q}{2\beta b} \qquad (5.43)$$

This implies an expected price for the product of:

$$P = \frac{a}{b} - \frac{Q}{2\beta b^2} \qquad (5.44)$$

The level of output that does maximize $\phi$ is:

$$Q^\star = \frac{2\alpha\beta b(bw\mu - a)}{1 - \alpha - 4\alpha\beta b^2 w\delta} \qquad (5.45)$$

The 'expected' value of $P$, $\bar{P}$, is derived by substituting (5.45) into (5.44):

$$\bar{P} = \frac{a}{b} - \frac{\alpha}{b}\left[\frac{bw\mu - a}{1 - \alpha - 4\alpha\beta b^2 w\delta}\right] \qquad (5.46)$$

Suppose that in a state of certainty the entrepreneur knows that the market price of his product will be $\bar{P}$. What amount would be produced? His *modus operandi* it may be assumed is the traditional one: he will choose $Q$ to maximize profits.

The resulting level of output is:

$$Q = \frac{\bar{P} - w\mu}{2w\delta} \tag{5.47}$$

Therefore:

$$Q^\star \gtreqless Q \text{ as: } 2\alpha\beta b\left[\frac{a - b\bar{P}}{\alpha}\right] \gtreqless \frac{\bar{P} - w\mu}{2w\delta} \tag{5.48}$$

$$Q^\star \gtreqless Q \text{ as: } (bw\mu - a) \gtreqless 0 \tag{5.49}$$

The sign of $Q^\star$ is affected by the sign of the left hand side of (5.49) and by the *values* of $\alpha, \beta$, the parameters of the $\phi$-function. A large value of $\beta$ will be an indicator of 'risk-aversion'. If $\beta$ is large then, *ceteris paribus*, $(bw\mu - a)$ must be negative to bring about $Q^\star > 0$. The higher is $\beta$, the greater is the likelihood that $Q^\star < Q$ at $\bar{P}$. At the margin a high weight, $2\beta\theta$, is attached to the $\theta$-index for any level of profit.

The uncertainty surrounding the chances of recouping the outlay on labour through a reasonable level of sales receipts acts to constrain the entrepreneur from hiring as much labour and producing as much output as he would have done had he been *certain* about $\bar{P}$; had he, in other words, assigned to it $\theta_{max}$, and a $\theta$ of zero to all other price-level candidates.

What about the entrepreneur's likely response to a sudden change in his Fixed Costs? Assume that:

$$\lambda = (P - wq)Q - FC \tag{5.50}$$
$$\phi = \alpha\lambda^2 + \beta\theta_\lambda \tag{5.51}$$
$$\theta = a - bP \tag{5.52}$$

We discover that:

$$\theta^\star = (a - bwq) - \frac{bFC}{Q} - \frac{b^2\beta}{2\alpha Q^2} \tag{5.53}$$

with $P^\star$ determined by equations (5.52) and (5.53). If, for the sake of exposition, we let:

$$\frac{a}{b} - 1 + \frac{b}{a}wq = 0 \tag{5.54}$$

the expression for $Q^\star$ is:

$$Q^\star = \frac{\beta b(1 - b^2)}{2\alpha(b^2 - a)FC} \tag{5.55}$$

A *ceteris paribus* increase in *FC* will have an impact on output; and a negative one at that. What would be the intuition behind that finding? More weight has been assumed to be attached in his ascendancy function by the entrepreneur to the level of profit *per se*. The increased Fixed Costs work to the detriment of profit: that deterioriation in profits could be aggravated by the entrepreneur's selecting a higher level of output with its impact on marginal (labour) costs, whilst there is no guarantee that the to-be-discovered price of the product will turn out to be sufficiently high to provide a revenue that will more than counter-balance the cost of the higher output.

Safety-First behaviour, embodied in the form of $\phi(.)$, dictates that the known, feasible, reduction in profits engendered by the rise in Fixed Costs is accommodated by a conservative choice of *P*, with a higher than otherwise credibility index. Output must then be lower.

## Investment in Real Capital

Suppose an entrepreneur has before him a range of new items of machinery out of which he is to choose one to install in his already existing factory or plant. The demand for his products has strengthened, looks likely to maintain its new level and suggests the possibility that expansion of output will be beneficial if he can only install a new piece of machinery to produce the extra output.

He has to decide whether the changes are that favourable, given the cost of purchase of any one machine. For any machine it may be imagined that he: forms a view as to its length of useful life; formulates the likely demand for the output of the to-be-acquired machine; estimates the receipts from the output; and conjectures about the variable costs (labour, raw materials, and so on) likely to be incurred in manufacturing those receipts. For a particular conjecture about each of these items there will emerge a net receipt figure for each year of (imagined) useful life of the relevant machine. These net receipts will be discounted by a rate of interest to produce the net present value figure. The difference between that figure and the (known) supply price or cost of purchase of the particular machine is then calculated: call this its net value.

For any machine there could be a series of net values, some of which could be negative as well as positive. That is to say, any one machine will hold out the expectation that it will produce losses. If for the machines under consideration some do offer, according to the entrepreneur's own expectations, just positive net value or gains (yields in excess of purchase cost) they must constitute the choice set: the remaining types of machine will be discarded.

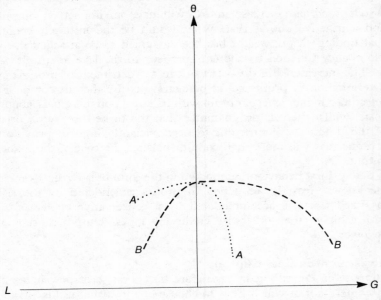

*Figure 5.4*

Suppose that there happen to be only two makes of machine that have the engineering properties that the entrepreneur needs for the manufacture of his product. Suppose also that both do seem to offer reasonable gains but also to lead to possible losses if labour and raw material inputs happen to assume the high values that the entrepreneur thinks they might possibly do, or if demand is not as buoyant as it might be.

The entrepreneur will not have at his disposal an objective probability distribution of those gains and losses on the two competing machines. It could be supposed that he does, of course; and, if he is then alleged to possess a 'utility' function over investment yields (rather than separately over gains and losses), his choice of machine to purchase could be determined by the Expected Utility Theory as is usually the case.

Alternatively, the existence of a probability density function for gains and losses could be postulated and Perspective Theory applied to this action-choice problem. If there is some kind of probability distribution for gains/losses, just over likely 'states of nature', Perspective Theory can solve this choice problem.

Let it be assumed, though, that the entrepreneur forms his own, subjective, assessment of the net values, the gains and losses, on

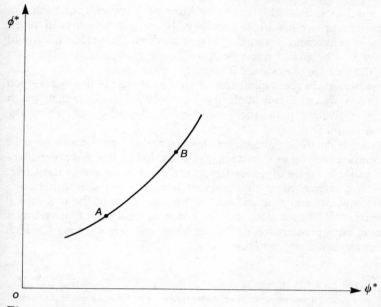

*Figure 5.5*

the machines; doing so by specifying a value of θ for the possible values of gains/losses that to him lie in the feasible range.

The outcome might look like the situation depicted in Figure 5.4. The gain and loss credibility functions have been drawn on the supposition that the expectational elements will be discrete. The θ-function *AA* relates to machine *A*. Machine *B* dominates machine *A*. It promises both higher ascendancy attractiveness and lower ascendancy unattractiveness. Should it be wished the θ-function can be replaced by some discrete probability function which maps into θ, one-to-one; the outcome is identical, *B* is chosen.

The θ-curves for *A* might lie inside those for *B*. In that case, the balance of the entrepreneur's perspective on the two uncertain prospects might lie with machine *A*: it all depends upon how loss-averse he is and how far the φ values of *A* and *B* differ. He could well be indifferent between *A* and *B*; they might share the same *P*-indifference curve as in Figure 5.5.

A further possibility is that the highest *P*-indifference curve, that is the highest perspective index that can be achieved, is the 'origin indifference curve'. The entrepreneur so views the conflicting prospects on the machines that his doubts about their bringing success to the firm lead him not only to be indifferent between the machines, but also to be indifferent between purchasing a machine and not making a purchase. If the psychic costs involved in the purchase and installation of new machines is included, I would expect that he would reject both machines; he would take the view that the balance of evidence favours the *status quo*.

Investment in real capital can be tackled along the lines developed for investment in financial claims. The only difference is that wealth or its equivalent here, the investment outlay, does not enter the picture explicitly.

As with portfolio investment, however, the model could be used to examine such factors as the degree of capital equipment diversification and the degree of diversification of investment across industries for any entrepreneur with a stock of wealth to invest in purchasing existing plants and machinery. Another extension of the real capital investment decisions would be concerned with the scale of investment that an entrepreneur might undertake in any one machine – which Perspective Theory can encompass.

## Notes

1   In effect, models of the Fisherian kind are one-period, not two-period, models.
2   I have assumed that the asset available for purchase is an irredeemable government bond; hence $R$ is the coupon divided by the bond price, at any point in time.
3   Incidentally, that double aspect of portfolio choice has been analysed rigorously in an Expected Utility framework by Drèze and Modigliani (1972).
4   The output equation is (for b = 1):

$$\frac{\beta^2}{2\alpha} - W\mu\beta Q^2 - W\delta\beta Q^3 - FC\beta Q - \beta W\mu Q^2 + 2\alpha W^2\mu^2 Q^4$$

$$+ 6\alpha W^2\delta\mu Q^5 + 2\alpha W\mu FC^3 - 2\beta W\delta Q^3 + 4\alpha W^2\delta^2 Q^6$$

$$+ 4\alpha W\delta FCQ^4 + \frac{\beta^2}{\alpha} = 0.$$

# PART III
# PERSPECTIVE THEORY AND ALTERNATIVE PARADIGMS

# 6 Perspective Theory Versus Shackle's Theory

I shall now outline the salient features of G.L.S. Shackle's (1952, 1961) model of decision-making under uncertainty (a full account is given in Ford 1983). These concern his new measure of uncertainty (potential-surprise) and the three central pillars he has constructed to describe how an individual makes a choice of strategy when the decision-taker has some degree of ignorance about the consequences of any action he chooses to pursue.

I shall also effect a comparison between Perspective Theory and the Shackle Theory, in terms of some specific elements of the two theories as well as in terms of their application to particular decision-problems.

## Shackle's Theory in Outline

Shackle's contention is that the probability calculus is an entirely inappropriate, indeed, irrelevant tool to employ as the formulation of a theoretical scheme designed to aid the choice of one course of action out of several mutually exclusive candidates, when uncertainty surrounding the outcome of any choice is unknown. The reasons: the act of choice is, or is likely to be, a unique one; it is not part of a 'serial, divisible experiment', when probabilities of eventualities could be found to be meaningful and relevant to the choice of experiment; and probability is a distributional variable. It must apply to a set of mutually exclusive, hence rival, hypotheses about the outcomes of a particular action-choice; being a variable, therefore, that sums to unity it is distributed across the range of outcomes. Consequently, any alterations in the constituents of the outcome-set must alter the probability attached to at least one of those outcomes.

Potential-surprise, or, more strictly, degrees of potential-surprise, replaces probability in Shackle's theory; and potential surprise is a non-distributional variable. It has a lower limit of zero for all individuals; and an upper limit, to represent the maximum degree of surprise that would be felt by the individual decision-taker if a specified outcome were to materialize, which can vary with individual temperament. To the series of consequences of a particular action the decision-taker is alleged to assign degrees of potential-surprise, $y$. In all instances where it is apposite, he forms a set of expectational elements (outcomes cum degrees of potential-surprise) for gains and losses separately.

Since, for each branch of the potential-surprise function, the outcomes are rivals, the gain elements, for example, are not encapsulated in some form of index which is based on a weighting or averaging of the competing expectational elements. According to Shackle's description of the thought-processes of the individual, as rival outcomes they will also be rivals jostling for the attention of the individual: only one gain outcome at the very best can occur. Viewed over gains and losses, even one gain outcome need not materialize.

The gain and loss expectational elements that capture the imagination of the individual assume an ascendancy in his mind. He maximizes an ascendancy stimulus or $\phi$-function, as it is alternatively labelled. The expectational elements of gain and loss have been reduced to one for gain and one for loss. *The rationale for the $\phi$-function is that it simplifies expectations.*

Both of those elements will, in general (but not always), consist of an outcome and an associated degree of potential-surprise. These elements are designated primary focus-elements. The two elements for gains and losses have then to be compared with the pairs of elements for all alternative strategies or action-choices.

To facilitate that comparison Shackle propounds the hypothesis that the primary focus-elements will be standardized, by the removal of their respective degrees of potential-surprise. The competing strategies will consist of pairs of just *monetary* outcomes, gains and losses. The resulting standardized focus-values for the strategies are ranked by means of a gambler indifference-map which epitomizes the individual's balancing of gains against (the risk of) loss.

Consider then a situation where the individual decision-taker happens to be an entrepreneur who is endeavouring to decide upon the type of machine that he should purchase to enhance his capital stock. He will estimate the likely gains ($G$) and losses ($L$) (positive and negative net present values) from investing in each of the available selection of machines. Imagine that his needs are so specialized, say he is a small tool manufacturer, that he is limited to a choice of two machines, one produced in Sweden ($S$) and one produced in the USA ($U$). Let the gain and loss branches of the expectation function, the potential-surprise function for $S$-machines, be as depicted in Figure 6.1.

The potential-surprise function $y(.)$ can assume an infinite number of forms: those drawn in Figure 6.1 are merely selected for illustrative purposes. The $\phi(.)$ need not be identical for gains and losses: indeed,

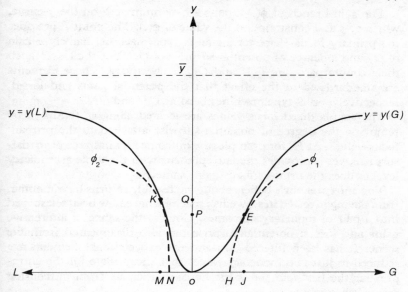

*Figure 6.1*

Shackle has mentioned the possibility that $\phi(L)$ could well differ from $\phi(G)$, depending upon and emphasizing the entrepreneur's attitude to risk (of loss). He has suggested that, in such an instance, $\phi$ for losses be defined by the Greek psi, $\psi$, as in my model:

> Hope and fear can co-exist in a man's mind ... even when both arise from a single issue and therefore cannot both be (objectively) well grounded. Yet we have drawn diagrams in which we measure $\phi$, whether derived from gain-elements or from loss-elements, upon the same axis. The reason for this is no more than the convenience of being able to show both branches of the *y*-curve on the same diagram. We might equally well (perhaps in strict logic it would be better) draw two separate diagrams, one for the 'gain' branch of the *y*-curve and one for its 'loss' branch, and use different symbols, say $\phi$ and $\psi$, for the stimulus derived from the gain-elements and from the loss-elements respectively. But the danger of any confusion which this precaution would be designed to eliminate seems hardly sufficient to warrant the extra complication. (Shackle 1952; 42).

Recall, also, that $\phi(.)$ depends solely upon an outcome and its associated degree of potential-surprise; and to the effect that the former has a positive, *ceteris paribus*, impact on $\phi$, the latter having a negative impact. Accordingly $\phi$-indifference curves can be represented by the curves $\phi_1$ and $\phi_2$ in Figure 6.1.

The gain branch of $\phi(.)$ attains a maximum at $E$ on the $y$-curve, which acts as a constraint on the value of $\phi(.)$. The point $E$ provides the primary focus-elements for an $S$-type machine, namely a gain of $OJ$ and a degree of potential-surprise of $OP$. For the loss-branch their counterparts are $OM$ and $OQ$, respectively. Those elements are standardized to the effect that the potential gains and losses, respectively, on $S$-type machines become $OH$ and $ON$.

The standardized focus-values are located along $\phi_1$ (and $\phi_2$), by removing the degree of potential-surprise attached to the primary focus-values. At $H$, for example, the outcome $OH$ has zero potential-surprise, yet it provides the entrepreneur with the same ascendancy level as does the primary focus-gain, namely $\phi_1$.

The entrepreneur's beliefs about the feasible returns he can obtain from having invested in a Swedish machine have now been telescoped into a pair of monetary outcomes. Gone is the range of alternative gains and losses; potential-surprise has also disappeared from the scene. It has been filtered out; and the expectational elements are reduced to just two monetary values that encapsulate for the entrepreneur the best and the worst he can anticipate from purchasing a Swedish machine.

For the USA machine the entrepreneur is regarded as pursuing the same routine. He epitomizes the prospects on the $U$-machine by two values for gain and loss. Those pairs of values are to be compared with the prospects of $OH$ and $ON$ for the $S$-machine: gain is balanced against the possible price (of loss) at which it can be attained, by the entrepreneur in terms of his preference for gambling. On the usual assumption that he is a risk, loss, averter, should there be a *ceteris paribus* improvement in the gains he believes could ensue from the purchase of a given type of machine, the more he will prefer that machine. Likewise, if his prospects become more sanguine by his reducing his estimate of the (standardized) focus-loss on a machine, *ceteris paribus*, his preference for that machine will be increased. In sum, the gambler-indifference curves can be depicted as I have drawn them in Figure 6.2.

The point $S$ represents the expectational prospects of the $S$-machine. Since the indifference curves will be ordered from the south-east to the north-west, if the focus-values for the $U$-machine lie along a gambler-indifference curve about $I_5$, the $U$-machine should be purchased. Although the $U$-machine is preferable to the $S$-machine, it also dominates the 'do-nothing solution', which is captured by $I_4$, the origin-indifference curve.

## Shackle's Theory and Perspective Theory
How does such a schema for arriving at the investment decision

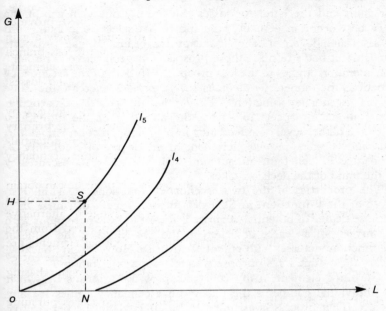

*Figure 6.2*

differ from Perspective Theory? It is clear how radically it differs
from the Expected Utility Theory: it and the Shackle theory *per
se* are mutually exclusive. It is also apparent that the Shackle theory
and Perspective Theory have some common features.

The main pillars of Perspective Theory are similar to those around
which the Shackle theory is constructed. Nevertheless they do differ.
Thus, let us recapitulate how the choice between $S$- and $U$-machines
would be taken by an entrepreneur if he adopted the approach proposed in Perspective Theory.

The potential-surprise functions would be replaced by $\theta$-functions,
expressing the credibility or degree of belief attached to any net
present value by the entrepreneur. Those $\theta$-functions diverge from
the $y$-functions by being credibility or belief functions and not potential surprise functions which can confuse surprise (possibility, in
effect, in Shackle's schema) and belief (or likelihood). The $\theta$-
functions, however, are postulated to possess separate branches. I
shall compare $\theta$ and $y$ later on but for the present will compare
the two theories given those concepts.

The choice over the uncertain outcomes is effected by the decision-
taker's maximizing two ascendancy functions, $\theta$ and $\psi$; the former

for gains and the latter for losses. Since only one gain can at the very best occur in actuality, the individual selects one gain, with its associated degree of belief, that captures for him the gain prospects available: it helps to place those prospects in perspective. The same consideration applies to the loss prospects. In both of the ascendancy functions the monetary outcomes, *ceteris paribus*, increase the value of the ascendancy functions. They raise the power of particular expectational prospects to attract the attention of the individual; to gain a higher level of ascendancy in his mind. In contrast, *mutatis mutandis*, a *ceteris paribus* increment in the degree of credibility of, or degree of belief in, an outcome will also raise its ascendancy in the mind of the decision-taker.

The properties of the two ascendancy functions are similar to those of the $\theta$-function, in Shackle's theory, except of course that, because degree of potential-surprise is meant to be synonymous with the inverse of a degree of belief, in the Shackle $\phi(.)$, the value of the function increases with potential-surprise. However, in Shackle's theory the $\phi$-function's purpose is to telescope expectations.

The third element in my construct provides a means by which the individual compares the maximum ascendancy values for any project. That process is assumed to be effected by the perspective function, whose value provides the perspective index for the relevant action-choice. The function does not exclude the degree of belief in the expectational elements that maximize the two ascendancy functions.

It is not very likely that the $\theta$-functions for gains and losses would be identical with the $y$-functions portrayed in Figure 6.1 – but let it be supposed that they were. In Perspective Theory the entrepreneur would base his perspective of $S$-machines on the combination of the pairs $(OJ, OP)$ and $(OM, OQ)$. In effecting a comparison between the merits of an $S$-machine and of a $U$-machine, the entrepreneur in Perspective Theory would never reduce the pairs to standardized units, such as $OH$ and $ON$ for gains and losses, respectively, for an $S$-type machine, whose expectational prospects are depicted in Figure 6.1. The action-choice made with regard to standardized focus-values in Figure 6.2 is now made with respect to $\phi_{max}$, $\psi_{max}$. The choice over $\phi_{max}$ and $\psi_{max}$ can be reduced to one over monetary gains and losses in Perspective Theory for certain choice decisions. However, those gains and losses are not standardized values; they are the 'primary' gains and losses, $OJ$ and $OM$.

The primary focus-elements would not place the entrepreneur on the same $P$-indifference curve as would the pair of standardized focus-outcomes unless $\phi(.)$, $\psi(.)$ and $P(.)$ were of special forms. Thus, if both $\phi(.)$ and $\psi(.)$ were additively separable and linear in both outcomes and degrees of belief, with the marginal ascendancy of outcomes being unity, and if $P$ was additively separable and linear in $\phi^\star$ and $\psi^\star$, then it would transpire that the level of the $P$-index for the primary focus-elements would be identical with that derived from their standardized counterparts.

As in Shackle's theory, $\phi(.)$, $\psi(.)$ and $P(.)$ will embody the decision-maker's attitude to risk. In the Shackle theory, however, one aspect of the risk-attribute of outcomes – their degrees of potential-surprise – has been omitted prior to the final choice of action at the level of the gambler-preference function. In general, the standardized focus-values will not even figure as possibilities in the entrepreneur's list of feasible outcomes: they will stand merely as 'certainty equivalents' of the primary focus-elements, having the same $\phi$-value, but they may not necessarily exist along the potential-surprise curve.

In a sense, the Shackle schema loses a degree of freedom (really, I suppose, two degrees of freedom) by its discounting of potential-surprise from the expectational characteristics of the opposing action-choices at the gambler-preference stage. This raises difficulties about the general applicability of the Shackle theory, especially with regard to portfolio selection. Except in virtually 'empty' situations, Shackle's theory has so far been shown to apply only to asset-diversification over *two* assets (*see* Egerton 1960; and Ford 1983). This is why Sir John Hicks (1967) has dismissed Shackle's Theory of Uncertainty and Expectations as offering a sensible means of rationalizing choice under uncertainty (*see* Hicks 1967: 121). Shackle himself (1952) has admitted that his theory is rather limited in that the best it can offer is two-asset portfolios – a result that he acknowledges is at variance with observed behaviour. He does offer suggestions as to why his schema might not account for asset choice, but those suggestions imply that his own paradigm is inappropriately structured. The suggestions are not admissible because they do require an alternative schema to be propounded to encompass portfolio selection.

To be specific: the Shackle schema reduces the decision-maker's expectational beliefs to just two magnitudes, a monetary gain and a monetary loss. If an individual's choice of asset portfolio is considered, the likely gains and losses per unit of investment in, say, a bond are reduced to two outcomes. This will be the case, *mutatis mutandis*, for all conceivable assets that the individual might purchase. Assuming that the only constraint that impinges upon his choice of portfolio is his level of wealth, the individual, it might be argued, will scale up the standardized focus-values, per unit of investment in any of the assets, to arrive at an assessment of the total (portfolio) gains/losses he believes will materialize from his placing all of his available wealth in any particular asset. By extension, he can calculate the gains and losses from having allocated his wealth in a pre-assigned fashion across a combination of the assets.

The gains and losses for any combination of asset holdings is a linear combination of the asset per unit gains – the weight applied to the latter being the (value of the) holdings of the respective assets. Through the gambler-preference map the investor's (implied) objective in the Shackle model is to locate the portfolio that promises the best combination of total standardized focus-values. In formal terms this means that: the constraint on the investor's attaining the highest possible gambler-preference indifference curve will be provided by a 'trading' line, an investment opportunity frontier, which embodies the maximum total standardized focus-gain the investor can anticipate for any value of total standardized focus-loss. Since both of those focus-values are linear in the value of asset holdings and so too is the wealth constraint, intuition would lead us to surmise that only two assets could be held (or need to be held) optimally in a portfolio. The set of asset holdings, whereby the best standardized focus-gain is obtained for any given standardized focus-loss and given wealth, being solved for from the last two variables, which are linear in the asset holdings.

A general proof of that proposition will be found in Ford (1983). For my current purposes I will accept that contention. Essentially it means that if it is assumed that the Shackle investor is contemplating investment in, say, two assets, the total standardized focus-values can be represented as follows:

$$G = g_A x_A + g_B x_B \qquad (6.1)$$
$$L = l_A x_A + l_B x_B \qquad (6.2)$$

Here the notation is: $G$ is total (from the spending of all wealth) standardized focus-gain; $L$ is total standardized focus-loss; $g_i$, $l_i$ are the standardized focus-gain and focus-loss, respectively, per unit of currency invested in asset $i$; and $x_i$ is the value of the holding of asset $i$. In Shackle's (1952) portrayal of the asset choice model assets are assumed to have, as it were, normalized coupon rates of zero; asset transactions incur no transaction costs; and there is no anticipated inflation.

With wealth $(W)$ defined as:

$$W = x_A + x_B \qquad (6.3)$$

equations (6.2) and (6.3) will provide values of $x_A$ and $x_B$ which depend upon $L$ and $W$, besides the focus-value elements of the individual assets. Insertion of the equations for $x_A$ and $x_B$ into the expression for $G$ yields the optimum investment frontier, the

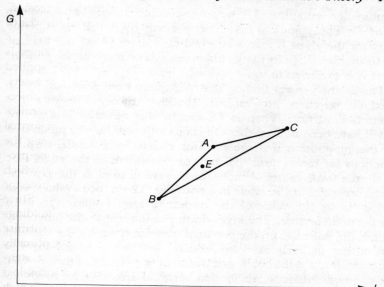

*Figure 6.3*

envelope equation $f(G,L) = 0$. That frontier is linear: its two bound-
ary points are when all wealth is allocated to the one asset or to
the other. On the supposition (of non-dominance) that $g_A > g_B$
and $l_A > l_B$ the frontier is upward sloping in $(G,L)$ space:

$$G = \frac{L(g_A - g_B) + W(l_A g_B - l_B g_A)}{l_A - l_B} \tag{6.4}$$

Now, suppose that a third asset exists, asset $C$, with characteristics
such that $g_C > g_A$ and $l_C > l_A$. There will be a linear $(G,L)$ frontier
connecting the points of total investment in asset $A$ and in asset
$C$.

The situation will be as depicted in Figure 6.3. The points $A$,
$B$, and $C$, respectively, depict the pair $(G, L)$ that obtain when
all of the investor's wealth is placed in those assets.

*Mutatis mutandis*, there will be a linear investment frontier that
can be drawn in Figure 6.3 to connect points $B$ and $C$. All points
within the resulting triangle must represent combinations of *three*
assets. However, none of those points will represent an optimum
portfolio of assets for a rational investor who acts according to the
Shackle schema. Why? The answer is immediate: any three-asset

combination is dominated by a two-asset combination. Thus consider point $E$. The point on $BA$ directly north of $E$ will be superior to $E$; for the given $L$ that is attached to $E$ more $G$ can be obtained north of $E$ on $BA$. In the gambler-preference map, *ceteris paribus*, more $G$ is preferred to less.

This is the general finding that transpires from formulating the portfolio selection problem in Shackle's theory following the Egerton–Ford line. What do I mean by that remark? Simply that it will have been noticed that the choice of portfolio was predicated on the supposition that the investor edited the potential-surprise functions for the 'returns' per unit of investment in the assets first of all: the focus-values of those assets were utilized as the expectational prospects of the assets in a portfolio. Those focus-values were scaled up by the value of the respective asset holding to obtain the portfolio picture. The investor, to put the matter the other way round, did not scale up the potential-surprise functions for the unit investment in each asset to obtain portfolio potential-surprise functions for, say, the holding of wealth in one asset, and then deduce the standardized focus-gain for that portfolio. Likewise, for combinations of asset holdings, the potential-surprise functions for the assets were not scaled up by the value of the holding of the respective assets and then all summed to provide the two branches of the surprise-functions for combinations of assets.

It would seem to be consonant with Shackle's emphasis on the psychology of decision-making and the individual's endeavour always to simplify complex expectational prospects. Shackle himself, however, tackles the asset choice question from the portfolio angle. He assumes that the investor can, and will, go through the process noted in the preceding paragraph. Nevertheless, he reaches the same conclusion as the one epitomized in Figure 6.3.

Shackle's (1952: Chapter IV) treatment of asset choice is couched in terms of assets as 'goods' and assets that have no coupon payment. Hence assets are compared over a unit-holding period, $(n - 1)$ to $(n)$, by reference to their prices, in effect the ratio of their expected price at $(n)$ compared with their spot price at $(n - 1)$; and it is at the date $(n - 1)$ that the entrepriser has to decide whether or not his current, inherited, portfolio is still an optimum one.

Initially, Shackle considers two goods, $B$ and $C$, whose price ratios (expected price : spot price) are labelled $a_B$ and $a_C$, respectively. To each price ratio there is a potential-surprise $(p)$ function (one for $a_i > 0$ and one for $a_i < 0$; $p_i = p_i(a_i)$). The investor is to decide by how much, if at all, he will increase his holdings of $B$ at the expense of $C$ or vice versa: that value change is denoted by $R$.

Of course, this characterization of the choice of portfolio composition is essentially the same as that wherein the investor is assumed to be choosing the best way of allocating his given wealth across any set of assets. So I shall retain Shackle's portrayal in order to be able to quote, in full, from his own analysis:

Let $\beta$ be the value of his initial holding of good $B$, let $\gamma$ be the value of his initial holding of good $C$, and let $R$, thought of as a variable hypothesis, be the value of those units of $C$ which he proposes, under different tentative plans, to exchange for units of $B$ ... Now let us write the ratio $a_B$ and $a_C$ in any pair of linked ratios, [ie where $p_B = p_C$] as functions $a_B = a_B(p)$ and $a_C = a_C(p)$ of the degree of potential-surprise associated with this pair of ratios. Then to *any given* degree $p = p_B = p_C$ of potential-surprise there will correspond a hypothesis of gain $x$ given by:

$$x = a_B(p)(\beta + R) + a_C(p)(\gamma - R) - \beta - \gamma,$$

so that:

$$\frac{\partial x}{\partial p} = \frac{da_B}{dp}\beta + \frac{da_C}{dp}\gamma + \left(\frac{da_B}{dp} - \frac{da_C}{dp}\right)R$$

Let us choose for $p$ that value which, at some one size of $R$, makes $x = g_P$, the primary focus-gain. Now it can perfectly easily happen ... that at this, or any, value of $p$ we have $da_B/dp = da_C/dp$. If this equality holds then $\partial x/\partial p$ is independent of $R$, and a change of the latter will leave unaffected the value of $p$ which gives $x = g_P$ ... we have $g_P$ as a *linear* function of $R$ ... Finally, if the shapes of the contour lines $\phi$ = constant are such (eg if, as is perfectly possible ... they are all identical) that when, as is true on our assumptions, $p$ is the same for all the values which $g_P$ can assume under changes of $R$ ... it follows that $g_S$, the *standardized* focus-gain, will be a linear function of $R$ ... By a parallel argument the other function, $h_S(R)$, can also quite easily be approximately linear. (Shackle 1952: 80-81; italics in original).

As a consequence, the investment frontier, $f(G,L) = 0$, for the two assets $B$ and $C$ will be linear. The limits of the frontier will represent the pair of $(G,L)$ from the investor's holding all of his wealth in the one asset or in the other. What about the multi-asset case? Shackle states that *the* investment frontier will consist of straight line segments such as $BA$ and $AC$ in Figure 6.3 and that points such as $E$ will be dominated, being pushed out of consideration by the investor (Shackle 1952: 89).

In Ford (1985) I accepted Shackle's own conclusions arguing that his use of a portfolio approach *per se* produced results synonymous with the Egerton (1960)–Ford (1983) approach; this indicated that the assumptions Shackle had made (concerning the slopes of portfolio potential-surprise functions) were innocuous and were, indeed, merely simplifying assumptions. Further research on this issue suggests that that was a slightly doubtful conclusion. In fact, if the portfolio approach is followed, at least a three-asset portfolio is attainable in the Shackle schema, rather than just one of two assets. However, it is not possible to produce mathematically general results that will establish a larger portfolio, although via numerical analysis it might be possible to generate one. The derivation of the optimum set of assets in the Shackle schema is so complicated that no topological method can be invoked to examine the feasibility of multi-asset portfolios. Even for the case of three assets, the mathematical form of the model has to be portrayed by the use of specific forms for the relevant behavioural functions; a general formulation becomes intractable.

The portfolio approach, adopted by Shackle himself, as I have noted, differs from that of Egerton–Ford through the fact that it operates with the potential-surprise functions for portfolios, derived from the 'scaling up' of the respective potential-surprise functions for a unit of investment in each of the assets by the holding of the relevant assets and summing them (for given degree of potential-surprise). Primary and standardized focus-values are derived, via the ascendancy functions, for each and every portfolio. Portfolios are then compared by means of the gambler-preference map.

Now, let the following assumptions be made:

$$\phi = -ay^2 + bG; \, a,b > 0 \tag{6.5}$$
$$\psi = -y^2 + cL^2; \, c > 0 \tag{6.6}$$
$$y_i = \alpha_i + \beta_i g_i; \, \alpha_i \leqslant 0, \beta_i > 0 \tag{6.7}$$
$$y_i = \gamma_i + \delta_i l_i; \, \gamma_i \leqslant 0, \delta_i > 0 \tag{6.8}$$

Here: $G$ denotes total gain on a portfolio; $L$ denotes total loss on a portfolio; $\psi(.)$ is the ascendancy function for losses, assumed to differ from $\phi(.)$, so that the asset-demand equations are not singular; $y$ is degree of potential-surprise; equations (6.7) and (6.8) represent the potential-surprise function for gain/loss per unit of investment in asset $i$, respectively; and $L$ is measured by its absolute value. To avoid undue complications caused by discontinuities I have assumed that the potential-surprise functions (6.7) and (6.8) could have, in principle, inner ranges in Shackle's sense that several outcomes per unit of investment in any asset could be assigned a zero degree of potential surprise. As far as $\phi(.)$ and $\psi(.)$ are concerned they permit the ascendancy indifference (contour) lines in $(y,G)$ and in $(y,L)$ space advocated by Shackle (1952, 1961).

I demonstrate in the Appendix to this chapter that a solution for an optimum set composed of three assets along the investment opportunity frontier (in total standardized focus $G$ and focus $L$ space) does exist. I also derive the best combinations of the three assets

*Table 6.1*

| L | G | U | $x_1$ | $x_2$ | $x_3$ |
|---|---|---|---|---|---|
| 15.0000 | 34.0681 | 11.1677 | 0.1248 | 2.6541 | 0.0211 |
| 16.0000 | 35.3638 | 11.1630 | 0.1115 | 2.4720 | 0.2165 |
| 17.0000 | 36.6657 | 11.1629 | 0.0986 | 2.2934 | 0.4080 |
| 18.0000 | 37.9737 | 11.1676 | 0.0859 | 2.1182 | 0.5959 |
| 19.0000 | 39.2878 | 11.1769 | 0.0736 | 1.9461 | 0.7803 |
| 20.0000 | 40.6078 | 11.1909 | 0.0615 | 1.7770 | 0.9615 |
| 21.0000 | 41.9338 | 11.2093 | 0.0497 | 1.6107 | 1.1396 |
| 22.0000 | 43.2656 | 11.2323 | 0.0381 | 1.4471 | 1.3148 |
| 23.0000 | 44.6032 | 11.2597 | 0.0268 | 1.2860 | 1.4873 |
| 24.0000 | 45.9466 | 11.2916 | 0.0156 | 1.1273 | 1.6571 |
| 25.0000 | 47.2956 | 11.3278 | 0.0047 | 0.9709 | 1.8244 |

*Parameter values:*

$\alpha_1 = -2.08;$  $\alpha_2 = -2.65;$  $\alpha_3 = -2.4;$
$\beta_1 = 0.08;$  $\beta_2 = 0.85;$  $\beta_3 = 0.4;$
$\gamma_1 = -1.23;$  $\gamma_2 = -2.5;$  $\gamma_3 = -4.2;$
$\delta_1 = 1.42;$  $\delta_2 = 3.83;$  $\delta_3 = 3.6.$
*Wealth* = 2.8 currency units.

*Optimum portfolio* $x_1 = 0.0047;$ $x_2 = 0.9709;$ $x_2 = 1.8244.$

---

that the investor should select if his gambler-preference function
is as follows:

$$U = \eta G + \varepsilon L ; \eta > 0, \varepsilon < 0 \qquad (6.9)$$

The results are catalogued in Table 6.1.

To derive these results it will be seen from equations (6.7) and
(6.8), together with their parameter values for the three assets, that
I have rescinded the assumption made by Shackle about the equivalence of the slopes of the portfolio potential-surprise functions at
the points where $\phi(.)$ is maximized. However, although this can,
contrary to my own previous opinion, permit a further degree of
asset diversification, it is not obvious that that degree could be
increased significantly. It has so far proved impossible, for example,
to extend the above specification to encompass the holding of more
than three assets; and I have experimented with innumerable specifi-
cations, discovering almost invariably that only at best a two-asset
portfolio is possible, since the $(G,L)$ frontier is still linear. It will
be observed, inevitably, that in the case of Table 6.1 that frontier
is non-linear (just!).

The experiments tried included alternative representations of $\phi(.)$, $\psi(.)$, $y_i = y_i(g_i)$ and $y_i = y_i(l_i)$. The general finding, if I can so describe it, since the results had necessarily to be derived from numerical models, was that the discounting of potential-surprise, the measure of uncertainty, from the final stage of action-choice, has reduced the degrees of freedom in the Shackle model. As with the Egerton–Ford approach, the Shacklean portfolio approach seems to produce (portfolio) standardized focus-values that are linear functions of the value of asset holdings. *Ergo*, only two assets can be held, optimally, on the $(G,L)$ frontier. After all, Shackle's assumptions in solving his model for asset choice using the portfolio approach do not seem to matter substantially: on balance, those assumptions were chosen with an acuity and ingenuity that permitted a short cut to be taken to solve the model.

Let us now turn to consider some other situations where decisions have to be taken under uncertainty and compare Perspective Theory with Shackle's theory. Some cases can be dealt with expeditiously. Thus, in Chapter 5 it has been shown how Perspective Theory, in either its probability or degree-of-belief versions, can be used to tackle a number of key decisions; such as output choice under demand (price) uncertainty and current saving decisions. I have indicated in Ford (1983) how the Shackle paradigm might be used to handle such decisions, and it does offer a solution to the choice of action in such circumstances, being able to embrace all of the topics discussed in Chapter 5 above.

Nevertheless the Shackle schema *per se* must produce different results, in principle, from Perspective Theory in all those instances where the uncertain prospects (whatever they might be), that confront decision-makers appear to them to promise either only gains or only losses. Consequently, in the case of all the topics covered in Chapter 5, except for the real investment decision, the Shackle framework will evaluate the action-choice of the individual differently from Perspective Theory, since in Shackle's theory, if only gains (or positive outcomes) are possible, the choice of action is determined, effectively, by the action strategy that promises the highest value of the ascendancy function. Even if it should happen that all the potential-surprise functions are the inverse of the $\theta$-function, the action-choices from the two theories must differ.

As a corollary, in general, the two theories will diverge in their analysis of lotteries to which I have referred in Chapters 1 and 2. However, because most of the lottery tickets there have only two outcomes, with the worst outcomes in each case virtually inseparable, Perspective Theory and Shackle's theory will lead to identical selection of lottery tickets which promise only gains. As with choice under uncertainty in the wider economic contexts mentioned in the preceding paragraph, where prospects offer only gains, the two theories will also produce divergent action-choices.

Strictly interpreted, of course, the Shackle theory cannot be applied to choice over lottery tickets. To do so we obviously have to convert the probabilities attached to the outcomes in the tickets to degrees of potential-surprise. The exercise becomes somewhat contrived, therefore, given the disparity in the ethos behind the two measures of uncertainty. Nevertheless, it is of some interest to pursue this line.

Thus, let us consider Problems 1 and 2 specified in Chapter 2 above, taken from Kahneman and Tversky's (1979) confirmation of the Allais Paradox.

*Problem 1*

| | |
|---|---|
| $A$: 2,500, 0.33 | $B$: 2,400, 1.0 |
| 2,400, 0.66 | 0, 0.0 |
| 0, 0.01 | |
| $N$: = 18% | $N$ = 82% |

*Problem 2*

| | |
|---|---|
| $C$: 2,500, 0.33 | $D$: 2,400, 0.34 |
| 0, 0.67 | 0, 0.66 |
| $N$: 83% | $N$ = 17% |

The modal preferences then were: $A \prec B$; $C \succ D$.

It would be legitimate in respect of lottery ticket $B$ to replace the probability of one by a zero degree of potential-surprise, and the zero probability by the maximum degree of potential-surprise, $\bar{y}$. Given Shackle's $\phi(.)$ it can follow readily that $B$ could be selected in preference to $A$; it could have a higher $\phi$-value than $A$, since the degree of potential-surprise 'equivalent' to the probability of 0.33 attached to the outcome 2,500 for $A$ exceeds zero, it could counterbalance the monetary gain advantage of $A$. Likewise, the $\phi$-value from $C$ could exceed that for $D$; there being no contradiction between the choices $B$ and $C$. The increase in the degree of potential-surprise now attached to the outcome 2,400 as we move from lottery ticket $B$ to lottery ticket $D$ can so reduce the $\phi$-value that it is below the (identical) maximum value for $A$ and $C$.

I have already noted that Perspective Theory can account for all the experimental choices over lotteries which promise gains or losses. Will the Shackle theory also be capable of explaining the choice over lottery tickets that offer only losses? If the examples presented in Chapter 2 are considered, it can be deduced again that the degrees of potential-surprise 'equivalent' to the probabilities could be such that all modal choices could be consistent with the

Shackle principle, which becomes merely 'choose the lottery ticket that minimizes the value of $\phi$'.

All of these points are speculative and heuristic. By construction, lottery ticket choice is not strictly amenable to analysis by Shackle's theory. Even if it could be transformed so that it at least appears to be usable in that context whilst it could produce the same action-choice, it need not do so. In general, and in instances where lotteries contain more than two outcomes, or where the worst (outcome, probability) combinations in all lotteries differ radically, the choice of lottery ticket will almost certainly differ for Perspective Theory and the Shackle theory. The lottery tickets described in Chapter 2 are of that nature, except for the 'Allais' example for Problem 1 for gains.

## The Axiomatization of Potential-Surprise and the Degree of Credibility

How does the degree of credibility compare with the uncertainty variable, degree of potential-surprise ($y$), advocated by Professor Shackle as an alternative to probability? My answer can best be provided by setting out the formal properties of potential-surprise by means of Shackle's own axioms. He lists these as follows:

1  An individual's degree of belief in a hypothesis can be thought of as consisting in a degree of potential-surprise associated with the hypothesis, and in another degree associated with its contradictory.

2  Degrees of potential-surprise can be zero or greater than zero. No meaning is assigned to a degree of potential-surprise less than zero.

   Degrees of potential-surprise are bounded above by that degree $\bar{y}$, called the *absolute maximum* of potential-surprise, which signifies the absolute rejection of the hypothesis to which it is assigned, absolute disbelief in the truth of the suggested answer to a question or the possibility of the suggested outcome of an 'experiment'.

3  Equality between the respective degrees of belief felt by an individual in two hypotheses will then require, for its expression in terms of potential-surprise, *two* statements, viz. that some given degree of potential-surprise is attached to both hypotheses, and that some given degree is attached to the contradictories of both.

4  The degree of potential-surprise associated with any hypothesis will be the least degree amongst all those appropriate to different mutually exclusive sets of hypotheses (each set con-

sidered as a whole) whose truth appears to the individual to imply the truth of this hypothesis.

5 All the members of an exhaustive set of rival hypotheses can carry zero potential-surprise.

6 When $H$ is any hypothesis, the degree of potential-surprise attached to the contradictory of $H$ is equal to the *smallest* degree attached to any rival of $H$.

7 Let $y_A^B$ be the degree of potential-surprise assigned to a hypothesis $B$ when $y_B^A$ is the degree assigned to a hypothesis $A$, and let $y_0$ be the degree assigned to $B$ when $y^A = 0$. Then $y^A_B$ is not greater than the greater of $y^A$, $y_0^B$.

8 Any hypothesis and its contradictory together constitute an exhaustive set of rival hypotheses.

9 At least one member of an exhaustive set of rival hypotheses must carry zero potential-surprise (Shackle 1952: 130-131; italics in original).

There are, as can be deduced, a number of points upon which the axiomatization of $\theta$ and of $y$ do differ. Consider first of all Axiom 5 in Shackle's formalization. He has stated that when a degree of potential-surprise of zero is assigned to any hypothetical outcome, that outcome, if it should occur, would produce no expression of surprise by the individual. Axiom 5 informs us that all of the rival outcomes can have a zero degree of potential-surprise.

Suppose that the set of rival hypotheses consists of only $H_1$ and $H_2$. Further, assume that $y_1 = 0$ and $H_2 = \bar{y}$. This has the corollary that $H_1$ is expected with certainty; there is no remotely feasible rival to that hypothesis. The further implication must be that zero degree of potential-surprise alone can represent the certainty of any hypothesis; Axiom 5 states that many hypotheses can carry that special degree of potential-surprise. Yet, if many do, zero potential-surprise cannot represent perfect certainty! Also, our axiom system excludes such a conundrum. Only one out of a set of competing hypotheses can be allocated $\bar{\theta}$.

Shackle's writings are not clear on this issue; yet he acknowledges explicitly that $\bar{y}$, the maximum degree of potential-surprise, represents for him the impossibility of the relevant event or hypothesis. Further he argues that:

To dismiss as unquestionably wrong some suggested answer to some question is an act of mind which we shall take to be one and the same thing for everyone, needing no definition ...

The essential choice [to capture degrees of uncertainty] we have to make is between ... a *distributional* and a *non-distributional* uncertainty variable. In the preceding ... we took as our departure the idea of certainty that some hypothesis is wrong. We did so because this idea has a plain direct meaning common, as we shall subsequently argue, to both distributional and non-distributional kinds of uncertainty-variable, while the idea of certainty that a hypothesis is right has a *simple* meaning only when we use a distributional uncertainty-variable, the idea of 'certainty of rightness' must be constructed (Shackle 1961: 47; italics in original).

Professor Shackle continues, somewhat paradoxically, to state that:

However, in order to discuss the concept of distributional uncertainty-variables, we shall assume that certainty of the rightness of a hypothesis is, like that of certainty of wrongness, a mental act or state familiar to everyone and needing no definition.

When a man is certain that a particular answer to some question is right, he means that that answer by itself exactly fills the vacant place constituted by the question, leaving no room for any other suggested answers (ibid.).

In that case $y = 0$ for one hypothesis and $\bar{y}$ for all other hypotheses must represent the case of certainty in Shackle's schema; and certainty (of rightness) as well as certainty of wrongness must be defined. Since $y = 0$ must represent certainty in such cases, it is true that certainty cannot be defined as 'an absolute' in Shackle's theory, because his Axiom 5 states that all members of a set of rival hypotheses can carry a zero degree of potential-surprise. Nevertheless, *all* the hypotheses cannot be imagined to be likely to come true with certainty; they are all perfectly possible, and no more.

If it is argued that for intuitive and logical reasons it is feasible, indeed meaningful, to have an absolute measure of the wrongness of an hypothesis, even with a non-distributional uncertainty-variable, then it is valid to argue that, alternatively, the certainty of rightness can be measured instead; or that *both* can be measured. In Shackle's case they are, even though there is an ambiguity over the measurement of certainty of rightness.

It is true that such a measure has to be constructed for a non-distributional variable, but so too does an indicator of certainty of wrongness. There is no logical inconsistency implied by my constructing such measures for both concepts. Any axiom system is, *ex definitione*, a set of postulates, a construct.

If we let $\bar{\theta} = 1$, to define the certainty of an hypothesis, and

$\theta = 0$ to define the impossibility of an hypothesis, we are not forced to axiomatize $\theta$ so that it does become the subjective probability concept of Savage (1954). Shackle gives the impression that he thinks that we are so constrained. He continues the above quotation as follows:

> He may then represent to himself this completeness by the integer one. If now that answer can be split into *additive components* which, when all taken together, come to the same thing as that answer, and if he wishes to represent to himself the share of any one component in the completeness achieved by the entire set of components, he will have to assign it some proper fraction, determined on a principle such that when all the fractions, one for each component, are listed, they sum to unity. Let us restrict $p$ to be a number such that $0 \leqslant p \leqslant 1$. Then when values of $p$ are assigned, on some principle which satisfies *the additive test* we have described, ... $p$ is serving as a distributional variable (Shackle 1961: 47-8; emphasis added).

It is important to note the emphasis I have imparted to this statement from Shackle. The general presumption in his argument seems to be that once an upper and a lower bound for an uncertainty-variable have been defined, that variable becomes a distributional variable, because the upper bound (representing certainty of rightness) must be applied to an exhaustive set of hypotheses (which, therefore, contain no residual hypotheses as Shackle calls them) and, since the set is imagined to occur with certainty, so must the sum of the individual components of that set. The number that is assigned to 'certainty' is irrelevant; it can be unity. In attaching a value of one to it Shackle is led to think of the uncertainty-variable as probability. However, it only has the same characteristics as probability if the additivity property invoked in Shackle's statement is valid: in that case Shackle's $p$ is defined to be a distributional uncertainty-variable.

The fact that his own uncertainty concept is not a distributional variable and does not possess a unique, unambiguous, conveyor of the rightness of any hypothesis, does not permit us to draw the conclusion that every non-distributional uncertainty-variable that might be suggested must also possess only one limit, certainty of wrongness. Neither does it, therefore, mean that if there is assumed to be an index of certainty (of rightness) that it must differ between individual decision-makers.

In Shackle's schema, for any set of exhaustive hypotheses about a specified question, the degree of potential-surprise (for the set) must be zero. There exists certainty about the rightness of the set. It has been shown that a zero of degree of potential-surprise cannot always be interpreted as denoting the property 'certainty of rightness'. Be that as it may; one of the points Shackle observes, which renders his notion of degrees of potential-surprise a non-distributional variable, is that the individual elements in the set of exhaustive hypotheses cannot be accorded a share of zero. Such an idea would be meaningless. So, within the set, the hypothetical outcomes can be assigned any degree of potential-surprise from zero to the maximum of $\bar{y}$.

Naturally, Shackle is entitled to devise his own set of axioms for an uncertainty-variable, but in my view the premise behind his implicit scale of zero for certainty of rightness is not valid; and the contradictions that are engendered by the absence of a unique measure of certainty of rightness in his axioms have led researchers to reject his whole schema. This has meant that many novel and valuable ideas have been dismissed out of hand.

On the first point these succinct observations from Ward Edwards (1945b) are apposite. These concern the relationship between objective and subjective probabilities, and have an immediate relevance here:

> The notion of objective probability is bounded by o and 1. Should a subjective probability scale be similarly bounded, or not? If not, then many different subjective probabilities will correspond to the objective probabilities (unless some transformation is used so that o and 1 objective probabilities correspond to infinite subjective probabilities, which seems unlikely). Considerations of the addition theorem ... have occasionally led people to think of a subjective probability scale bounded at o but not at 1. This is surely arbitrary. The concept of absolute certainty is neither more nor less indeterminate than is the concept of absolute impossibility.
>
> Even more drastic logical problems arise in connection with the addition theorem. If the objective probability of event $A$ is $P$, and that of $A$ not occurring is $Q$, then $P + Q = 1$. Should this rule hold for subjective probabilities? Intuitively it seems necessary that if we know the subjective probability of not-$A$, and the only reasonable rule for figuring it out is subtraction of the subjective probability of $A$ from that of complete certainty ... Only for a subjective probability scale identical with the objective probability scale will the subjective probabilities of a collection of events, one of which must happen, add up to 1 ...
>
> One way of avoiding these difficulties is to stop thinking about a scale of subjective probabilities and, instead, to think of a weighting function applied to the scale of objective probabilities according to their ability to control behaviour ... *There is no reason why such weighted probabilities should add up to 1 or should obey any other simple combinatory principle* (Edwards 1954b: 397–8; emphasis added).

My degrees of credibility are not the same as the weights advocated by Edwards, and by those who have followed him in formalizing his ideas into Prospect Theory. Neither is my suggested credibility index propounded as a controller of behaviour and hence as an *ex post* rationalization of experimental results.

We now turn, briefly, to the other point related to the absence of a unique 'certainty of rightness' indicator in Shackle's theory: that theory leads to a confusion between perfect possibility and degree of belief. If an hypothesis, *H*, is regarded by the individual as something that would not surprise him at all if it should turn out to be the correct outcome, it must be assigned a zero degree of potential-surprise. So perfect possibility maps into a degree of potential-surprise of zero; but a zero degree of surprise does not map automatically into some degree of belief.

This was a major thrust in Sir Charles Carter's (1950, 1953) criticisms of potential-surprise, which were the first critical assessment of the first and second editions of Shackle's *Expectation in Economics* (1952). It was also an issue on which Dorfman (1955) criticized Shackle in his review of the Liverpool Symposium on Uncertainty and Business Decisions (Carter, Meredith and Shackle (eds) 1954). He puts matters in a nutshell:

> Carter also questions Shackle's attitude toward the relationships between those two slippery concepts 'degree of surprise' and 'degree of belief'. The problem is that while both of these concepts are intuitively appealing substitutes for mathematical probability, they are almost indefinable; reasoning based on the one contradicts reasoning based on the other, and no accepted basis for reconciling the two exists. The vagueness of the relationship between the two is illustrated by the fact that a man using a telephone has a low degree of belief in getting a wrong number but also a low degree of surprise if he does. (Dorfman 1955).

This suggests that the very concept of degree of potential-surprise cannot be interpreted to produce any (meaningful) measure of certainty (of rightness). Professor Shackle's retort, whilst at first sight seeming like an *ignoratio elenchi*, is a direct answer, but it serves, I feel, only to illustrate how contorted potential-surprise is as an alternative to probability. In effect, he invokes Axiom 1 of his system to answer Dorfman. If it is assumed that either the right or the wrong telephone number will be obtained, a zero degree of potential-surprise in obtaining the right number (as the least surprising rival hypothesis to obtaining the wrong number) means that the degree of belief assigned to obtaining the wrong number is also zero. The degree of belief in an hypothesis is alleged (one-to-one) to be related to potential-surprise; but to the potential-surprise attached to the competing hypothesis!

In his endeavour not to define an uncertainty-variable that is defined over an interval, the limits of which represent certainty of rightness and wrongness, and one which is implicitly cast in terms of dis-belief (rather than belief),[1] Shackle has produced a concept that is ambiguous and paradoxical. The difficulties in understanding it are not merely ones of semantics as he has frequently suggested to his critics (Shackle 1961).

Nevertheless the ethos behind his desire to produce a new uncertainty-variable I accept entirely. There are grounds for replacing probability, subjective or objective, as an uncertainty-variable. In most situations that require decisions to be made the individual, household unit, business man, investment manager, does have to make choices, with incomplete knowledge. Introspectively, degrees of credibility measures are used to epitomize the weight that can be placed on possible outcomes. Those weights need not, and I would suggest do not, always sum to a fixed number, such as unity. Several hypotheses can have the same standing in the mind of the individual and be unaffected by his believing that the empirical evidence now enables other hypothetical outcomes to be possible, hitherto thought to have a zero degree of credibility. The fact that sets of outcomes will be seen as consisting of mutually exclusive elements will mean that there is no meaning to be attached to adding their respective degrees of credibility: they cannot be envisaged as being constrained by the credibility of the set *per se*. Even if the individual is offered the choice of uncertain prospects, such as lottery tickets, to which 'objective' probabilities are attached, so that he decides not to calculate his own credibility indices, I have propounded the theory that, since the Shacklean view that probability is only relevant to seriable experiments is unimpeachable, the individual will act on the knowledge that only one outcome can occur; events will not be added or averaged. So for reasons associated with the distributional nature of probability and with its dubious relevance to 'unique' or 'next' decisions, I advocate the use of an alternative uncertainty-variable and an alternative theory of decision-making. Where probability indicators are available and utilized, they are only used in the way described by Perspective Theory.

I suggest, however, that Shackle's own uncertainty-variable is not entirely appropriate and that my own degree of credibility concept circumvents the conundrums present in degrees of potential-surprise. In addition to the latter and with little supporting argument, Shackle claims that it is almost self-evident that it is feasible to define degrees of surprise. Common usage of the notion of surprise might, however, lead one to the conclusion that one is either surprised or not surprised; that surprise is an absolute concept. In using my uncertainty-variable I further suggest that $\bar{\theta}$ can be set at unity; but this does not exclude the possibility that $\bar{\theta}$ can differ from that magnitude and between individuals. Like Shackle, though, despite the fact that

I have used degree of belief and degree of credibility for θ, it should be seen to be a credibility index, as intimated earlier in this chapter: the use of credibility makes it easier to see how a non-distributional uncertainty-variable can exist.[2]

## Notes

1  About a set of mutually exclusive hypotheses, in summary of his approach, he writes:

> To believe in one of these answers is therefore to disbelieve in the others. By contrast it is *not* true that to disbelieve in one answer is to believe in the others. Thus, it seems more natural . . . in order to label various answers with this status or that in relation to 'certainty of rightness' or 'certainty of wrongness' to use a variable expressing *disbelief*. Zero potential-surprise expresses *zero* disbelief . . . To invert a problem is a well-known resource of the mathematician. We too, in adopting as our uncertainty-variable a measure of *disbelief*, are in a way inverting our problem, and we are thereby guaranteeing our solution against any attempt to turn it back into a distributional variable. (Shackle 1961: 74-5; italics in original).

2  Shackle argues more strongly than I would but his view is that:

> We must, therefore, distinguish sharply between the notion, on the one hand, of a man's degree of actual belief in some hypothesis, and on the other hand, of the degree of 'believability' which he accords it. To believe positively that some hypothesis is right is *pro tanto* to dismiss all rival hypotheses as wrong. But to regard a hypothesis as credible or plausible is not necessarily to pass any judgement on the credibility or plausibility of other hypotheses: the insufficiency of any man's knowledge, of principle and of facts . . . leaves room for him to accept as believable very many diverse and mutually contradictory hypotheses about any one matter. (Shackle 1961: 75).

# Appendix: Three Asset Diversification in Shackle's Model: A General Proof

To recapitulate, I assume that:

$$\phi = -ay_G^2 + bG; \; a,b > 0 \tag{A6.1}$$
$$\psi = -y_L^2 + cL^2; \; c > 0 \tag{A6.2}$$
$$(y_i)g = \alpha_i + \beta_i g_i; \; \alpha_i \leqslant 0, \; \beta_i > 0 \tag{A6.3}$$
$$(y_i)_l = \gamma_i + \delta_i l_i; \; \gamma_i \leqslant 0, \; \delta_i > 0 \tag{A6.4}$$

Now, let:

$$x' = [x_1, x_2, \ldots, x_n] \tag{A6.5}$$

The consequence is that using (A6.1), (A6.3) and (A6.5) it is discovered that, for given $x$:

$$SFG = (b/4a)x'\Omega x - x'A \tag{A6.6}$$

where:

$$\Omega = \begin{bmatrix} 1/\beta_1 & 1/\beta_1\beta_2 & \cdots & 1/\beta_1\beta_n \\ 1/\beta_2\beta_1 & 1/\beta_1{}^2 & \cdots & \\ . & & & \\ . & & & \\ . & & & \\ 1/\beta_n\beta_1 & & \cdots & 1/\beta_n{}^2 \end{bmatrix} \tag{A6.7}$$

and

$$A = \begin{bmatrix} \alpha_1/\beta_1 \\ . \\ . \\ . \\ \alpha_n/\beta_n \end{bmatrix} \tag{A6.8}$$

with $SFG$ denoting standardized focus-gain.

Additionally, using (A6.2), (A6.4) and (A6.5), for given $x$:

$$SFL = x'\Gamma x[((1/c^2)/c)\, x'\Delta x + 1]/1 - cx'\Delta x \tag{A6.9}$$

Here:

$$\Gamma = \begin{bmatrix} (\gamma_1/\delta_1)^2 & \gamma_1\gamma_2/\delta_1\delta_2 & \cdots & \gamma_1\gamma_n/\delta_1\delta_n \\ \gamma_2\gamma_1/\delta_2\delta_1 & (\gamma_2/\delta_2)^2 & \cdots & \\ \vdots & & & \\ \gamma_n\gamma_1/\delta_n\delta_1 & & \cdots & (\gamma_n/\delta_n)^2 \end{bmatrix} \tag{A6.10}$$

$$\Delta = \begin{bmatrix} 1/\delta_1{}^2 & 1/\delta_1\delta_2 & \cdots & 1/\delta_1\delta_n \\ 1/\delta_2\delta_1 & (1/\delta_2)^2 & \cdots & \\ \vdots & & & \\ 1/\delta_n\delta_1 & & \cdots & (1/\delta_n)^2 \end{bmatrix} \tag{A6.11}$$

with *SFL* denoting standardized focus-loss. It is now from equations (A6.8) and (A6.9) using the wealth constraint:

$$W = i'x;\, i' = [1\ 1\ \ldots] \tag{A6.12}$$

that the optimum set of assets on the frontier, and hence the frontier itself, is to be discovered.

An analytical solution can be obtained if we assume that:

$c = 1$ and

$$A = k_1\beta + k_2 i \tag{A6.13}$$

where

$$\beta = [1/\beta_1, 1/\beta_2, \ldots, 1/\beta_n]' \tag{A6.14}$$

and $k_1$, $k_2$ are scalars. The assumption that c is unity reduces the degree of non-linearity in the analysis. Assumption (A6.13) has a similar effect as we shall see.

If we let $z = b/4a$ the Lagrangean is:

$$\mathscr{L} = zx'\Omega x - A'x - \lambda\,[(x'\Delta x - 1)L + x'\Gamma x] - \mu(x'i - W) \tag{A6.15}$$

with $\lambda$ and $\mu$ being the two Lagrangean multipliers and $L$ denoting *SFL*.

Hence we need to solve:

$$2(z\Omega - \lambda(L\Delta + \Gamma))x = A + \mu i \tag{A6.16}$$
$$x'(L\Delta + \Gamma)x = L \tag{A6.17}$$
$$x'i - w = 0 \tag{A6.18}$$

for $x$, $\lambda$ and $\mu$.

We note that

$$\Omega = \beta\beta'; \Delta = \delta\delta'; \text{ and } \Gamma = \gamma\gamma' \tag{A6.19}$$

where $\beta$ is as defined in (A6.14) and:

$$\delta = [1/\delta_1, 1/\delta_2, \ldots, 1/\delta_n]' \text{ and}$$
$$\gamma = [\gamma_1/\delta_1, \gamma_2/\delta_2, \ldots, \gamma_n/\delta_n]' \tag{A6.20}$$

Now define:

$$\left. \begin{array}{l} y_1 = \sqrt{z}\ \beta'x; \\ y_2 = \sqrt{L}\ \delta'x; \\ y_3 = \gamma'x; \end{array} \right\} \tag{A6.21}$$

thus:

$$y = M'x \tag{A6.22}$$

where:

$$M = (\sqrt{z}\beta \quad \sqrt{L}\delta \quad \gamma) \tag{A6.23}$$

We can then write:

$$2(z\Omega - \lambda(L\Delta + \Gamma))x = 2M(I - (1 + \lambda)N)y \tag{A6.24}$$

with:

$$N = \begin{bmatrix} 0 & 0 & 0 \\ 0 & 1 & 0 \\ 0 & 0 & 1 \end{bmatrix} \tag{A6.25}$$

Since:

$$(I - (1 + \lambda)N)^{-1} = [I - (1 + 1/\lambda)N] \tag{A6.26}$$

defining:

$$p = M^{-1}A; q = M^{-1}i; \text{ and } \bar{\lambda} = 1 + 1/\lambda \tag{A6.27}$$

Using (A6.24) to (A6.27), (A6.16) to (A6.18) can be rewritten as: solve the following system of equations for $y_1, y_2, y_3, \lambda$ and $\mu$:

$$\begin{array}{l} y_1 = 1/2(p_1 + \mu q_1) \\ y_2 = 1/2(1 - \bar{\lambda})(p_2 + \mu q_2) \\ y_3 = 1/2(1 - \bar{\lambda})(p_3 + \mu q_3) \\ y_2^2 + y_3^2 = L \\ y_1 q_1 + y_2 q_2 + y_3 q_3 = W \end{array} \tag{A6.28}$$

An analytical solution to equation (A6.28) can be derived if it is assumed:

$$p_2/q_2 = p_3/q_3 \tag{A6.29}$$

Since this implies that:

$$\begin{vmatrix} 1 & p_1 & q_1 \\ 0 & p_2 & q_2 \\ 0 & p_3 & q_3 \end{vmatrix} = 0 \qquad (A6.30)$$

it further implies from the definition of $M$ that:

$$|M^{-1}(Me_1 \ A \ i)| = 0 \qquad (A6.31)$$

where:

$$e_1 = [1 \ 0 \ 0]'$$

Therefore:

$$|\beta \ A \ i| = 0 \qquad (A6.32)$$

and hence, in general:

$$A = \sqrt{z}k\beta + l_i \qquad (A6.33)$$

where $k$ and $l$ are constants. In effect, (A6.32) and (A6.33) are equivalent to equation (A6.13).

Utilizing the information in (A6.33) to rewrite $P$, given in equation (A6.27), it is found that:

$$y_1 = 1/q_1(W - L(q_2^2 + q_3^2)^{\frac{1}{2}} \qquad (A6.34)$$
$$y_2 = (q_2\sqrt{L})/(q_2^2 + q_3^2)^{\frac{1}{2}} \qquad (A6.35)$$
$$y_3 = (q_3\sqrt{L})/(q_2^2 + q_3^2)^{\frac{1}{2}} \qquad (A6.36)$$
$$\mu = [(2y_1 - (k/\sqrt{z})]/q_1) - l \qquad (A6.37)$$
$$\lambda = (-(l + \mu)q_2)/2y_2 \qquad (A6.38)$$
$$x = (M')^{-1}y \qquad (A6.39)$$
$$G = y_1^2 - (k/\sqrt{z})y_1 - lW \qquad (A6.40)$$
$$dG/dL = (k_1 - 2y_1)(q_3y_3/2q_1L) \qquad (A6.41)$$

In the specific example I have developed I have been able, therefore, to generate the general expression for the investment opportunity frontier. Note that the frontier is non-linear.

It is now possible to derive the optimum holding of the three assets by positing the form of $U(.)$. Adopting the same form as hitherto, namely:

$$U = \eta G + \varepsilon L; \ \eta > 0, \varepsilon < 0 \qquad (A6.42)$$

utilizing assumption (A6.13) it is discovered that:

$$y_1 = \frac{W - q_2y_2 - q_3y_3}{q_1} \qquad (A6.43)$$

$$y_3 = \frac{q_2(1 - y_2^2)}{q_3y_2} \qquad (A6.44)$$

$$y_2 = \frac{-2q_2(\varepsilon q_1^2 - \eta q_3^2)}{\eta q_3[q_1(p_1 q_3 - p_3 q_1) - 2q_3 W]} \tag{A6.45}$$

$$SFL = (q_2/q_3)^2 \frac{(1 - y_2^2)}{y_2^2} \tag{A6.46}$$

$$SFG = y_1^2 - p'y \tag{A6.47}$$

with $x$ defined by equation (A6.39) given the $y$-vector from equations (A6.43) to (A6.45).

# 7 Prospect Theory and Regret Theory in Brief

This chapter provides an overview and partial critique of the two theories that have been developed to explain behaviour in the lottery experiments reported over the past thirty years, which the Expected Utility model cannot do. These are known as Prospect Theory and Regret Theory. The former is derived directly from an analysis of the laboratory experiments – an inductive theory. Regret Theory is partly derived by an integrative method from the behaviour of the participants in the laboratory experiments. It was prompted by that behaviour and is a theory that can account for it. The theory is similar to a utility variant of the Savage (1951) Minimax Regret decision criterion.

Both of these theories are dependent upon (objective) probabilities; even though Prospect Theory uses 'decision weights' that decision-makers are alleged to form on the basis of the objective probability attached to any particular outcome. Those weights, pseudo- 'subjective' probabilities (they do not sum to unity) are used to weight the Von Neumann–Morgenstern utility for each outcome in a prospect (that is, the consequences of a specified action-choice, or strategy) to arrive at its 'expected' utility index, rather than using the relevant objective probabilities as weights, which is the procedure in the Expected Utility Theory.

Also, both theories have to date been developed only in the context of the very simple choices that are tacit in the selection of one 'gamble' or another, usually over pairs of prospects only, with the gambles themselves involving a maximum of only three outcomes (including the zero outcome) in the case of Prospect Theory. It is doubtful whether either theory could be applied to the usual panoply of choices that have to be explained under uncertainty in economics.

Regret Theory differs from Prospect Theory in that it does not assume that the decision-maker calculates an index to encapsulate the prospects available from some action-choice by weighting or 'averaging' all of the outcomes in a prospect. In that regard, unlike Prospect Theory, it departs from the essence of the approach embodied in the Expected Utility Theory. A decision-maker does not carry in his mind all the aspects of a prospect: and his index of the 'utility' of any prospect depends upon the regret he would feel as a consequence of the other prospect's having materialized. For two prospects, the core of Regret Theory is best given by the following extract from Loomes and Sugden:

> Our first assumption is that for any given individual there is a *choiceless utility function* $C(.)$, unique up to an increasing linear transformation, which assigns a real-valued utility index to every conceivable consequence.
> The significance of the word 'choiceless' is that $C(x)$ is the utility that the individual would derive from the consequence $x$ if he experienced it *without having chosen it*. For example, he might have been compelled to have $x$ by natural forces, or $x$ might have been imposed on him by a dictatorial government. Thus – in contrast to the Von Neumann–Morgenstern concept of utility – our concept of choiceless utility is defined independently of choice. Our approach is utilitarian in the classical sense. What we understand by 'choiceless utility' is essentially what Bernouilli and Marshall understood by 'utility' – the psychological experience of pleasure that is associated with the satisfaction of desire . . .
> Now suppose that an individual experiences a particular consequence as the result of an act of choice. Suppose that he has to choose between actions $A_1$ and $A_2$ in a situation of uncertainty. He chooses $A_1$ and then the $j$th state of the world occurs. He therefore experiences the consequence $x_{1j}$. He now knows that, had he chosen $A_2$ instead, he would be experiencing $x_{2j}$. Our introspection suggests to us that the psychological experience of pleasure associated with having the consequence $x_{1j}$ in these circumstances will depend not only on the nature of $x_{1j}$ but also on the nature of $x_{2j}$. If $x_{2j}$ is a more desirable consequence than $x_{1j}$, the individual may experience *regret*; he may reflect on how much better his position would have been, had he chosen differently, and this reflection may reduce the pleasure that he derives from $x_{1j}$. Conversely, if $x_{1j}$ is the more desirable consequence, he may experience what we shall call *rejoicing*, the extra pleasure associated with knowing that, as matters have turned out, he has taken the best decision . . . This concept of regret resembles Savage's (1951) notion in some ways, but it will emerge that our theory is very different from his minimax regret criterion.
> We shall incorporate the concepts of regret and rejoicing into our theory by means of a *modified utility function*. Suppose that an individual chooses action $A_i$ in preference to action $A_k$, and that the $j$th state of the world occurs. The actual consequence is $x_{ij}$ while, had he chosen differently, $x_{kj}$ would have occurred. We shall write $C(x_{ij})$ as $c_{ij}$ and we shall then say that the individual experiences the *modified utility* $m_{ij}^k$ where:

$$m_{ij}^k = M(c_{ij}, c_{kj}).\tag{1}$$

> The function $M(.)$ assigns a real-valued index to every ordered pair of choiceless utility indices. The difference between $m_{ij}^k$ and $c_{ij}$ may be interpreted as an increment or decrement of utility corresponding with the sensations of rejoicing or regret . . . it is natural to assume . . . that if $c_{ij} = c_{kj}$ then $m_{ij}^k = c_{ij}$: if what occurs is exactly as pleasurable as what might have occurred, there is neither regret nor rejoicing. It is

equally natural to assume that $\partial m_{ij}^k/\partial c_{kj} \leqslant 0 \ldots$ We also make the uncontroversial assumption that $\partial m_{ij}^k/\partial c_{ij} > 0$: that, other things being equal, modified utility increases with choiceless utility.

Our theory is that the individual chooses between actions so as to maximize the mathematical expectation of modified utility. We may define the *expected modified utility* $E_i^k$ of action $A_i$, evaluated with respect to action $A_k$, by:

$$E_i^k = \sum_{j=1}^{n} p_j m_{ij}^k. \tag{2}$$

Faced with a choice between $A_i$ and $A_k$, the individual will prefer $A_i$, prefer $A_k$, or be indifferent between them according to whether $E_i^k$ is greater than, less than or equal to $E_k^i$.

Why, it may be asked, do we assume that people maximize the mathematical expectation of modified utility? Principally because this is a simple assumption which yields implications consistent with empirical evidence. We do not claim that maximizing expected modified utility is the only objective that is consistent with a person being rational (Loomes and Sugden 1982: 807-808).

It is possible, as Loomes and Sugden have done, to show that this model is capable of explaining away the experimental findings of Kahneman and Tversky (1979). However, they also note that the model is not compatible with the experiments of Bell (1981) and Fishburn (1981).

It will be recalled that the Expected Utility of any action-choice, strategy or prospect can be written as:

$$\Sigma\, u(a_{ij})\, \Pi_j i \tag{7.1}$$

where: $u(.)$ is the Von Neumann–Morgenstern utility function over outcome; $a_{ij}$ is the outcome in the $j$th state of nature for action-choice $i$; and $\pi_j$ is the probability of occurrence of state of nature $j$ (*see* Chapter 1 and its Appendix).

Prospect Theory does not depart radically from Expected Utility Theory. It postulates that the $\pi_j$ in equation (7.1) will be replaced by weights, $w$, which depend upon $\pi_j$, that is, $w_j = w(\pi_j)$, with the $\Sigma w_j < 1$, *ex hypothesi*. The precise form the resulting index assumes, since, *ex definitione*, it cannot now be labelled $E(U)$, depends upon whether any prospect confronting the individual decision-maker consists of either 'gains' or 'losses', and whether, for a prospect that does not promise losses, the outcomes are non-positive or strictly positive. The Index $E(U)$ is replaced by $V(.)$, with the $u(.)$ constituent of $E(U)$ defined as $v(.)$. Prospect Theory has been so-named by Kahneman and Tversky (1979) although their main point, that the action-choice index is non-linear in probabilities, in contrast to the corollary of the Von Neumann–Morgenstern axioms, was one of the major conclusions Edwards (1954c, 1955) drew from the several laboratory tests he performed of expected Utility Theory. His proposed theory which he did not explicate, it is true, was that the choice-index would be the same as the right hand side of equation (7.1), with $\pi_j$, replaced by $w_j = w(\pi_j)$. A study of Edwards does suggest that he perceived the utility of outcomes $u(.)$ to be different from that in the theory of Von Neumann–Morgenstern: it seems that Edwards envisaged the utilities to be derived from the attractiveness of outcomes under certainty; whereas, the essential attribute of the Von Neumann–Morgenstern utility function, implied as it is by their axioms, is that it is construed under uncertainty, from choice of lotteries (*see* Appendix to Chapter 1). In essence, to be pedantic, this would mean that Edwards's choice index would be a non-linear reformulation of the first Expected Utility model, that proposed by Daniel Bernouilli (1738); the latter's choice-index being one in Expected Utility, but with the $u(.)$ in equation (7.1) taken to be utility from outcomes (returns, wealth, additions to wealth . . .) obtainable under certainty.

Schoemaker (1982), in an excellent survey of the 'state of the arts' in regard to Expected Utility, its variants and the empirical evidence, states that the Kahneman–Tversky specification of Prospect Theory is identical with the choice-index posited by Edwards. However, a perusal of Kahneman and Tversky suggests that, on pedagogic grounds, this might not be so. The $v(.)$, utility of outcomes, or what they call the *value* function, is seen initially by Kahneman and Tversky as deriving from outcomes that are known to be obtainable under certainty. However, they state during their exposition of $v(.)$ that:

> The above hypothesis regarding the shape of the value function was based on responses [of subjects in their laboratory experiments] to gains and losses in a riskless context. We propose that the value function which is derived from risky choices shares the same characteristics, as illustrated in the following problems [lottery ticket choices presented to their subjects] (Kahneman and Tversky 1979: 278).

The Kahneman–Tversky theory is developed, as noted previously, in the light of their own laboratory experiments (some of which have been summarized in Chapter 2) which produced intrinsically identical results to those of previous researchers, beginning with Edwards (1953, 1954c, 1955). The theory is proposed, therefore, against the special background of those experiments: their own and those of Allais, and some of those of Edwards, were based on extremely simple choices being presented to participants, in the form of choice of lottery tickets; tickets that promised either gains or losses; all tickets having objective probabilities assigned to their

respective outcomes which could be taken as sacrosanct by participants. Hence they were selecting one fixed-odds bet or another.
The probabilities, therefore, could be taken as meaningful. Also,
very importantly, the choices confronting the subjects in the experiment were not only gambles in the everyday meaning of the term,
but simple gambles each described by a minimal range of alternatives.
In the words of Kahneman and Tversky:

> The present formulation is concerned with simple prospects of the form
> $(x,p; y,q)$, which have at most two non-zero outcomes. In such a prospect,
> one receives $x$ with probability $p$, $y$ with probability $q$, and nothing with
> probability $1 - p - q$, where $p + q \leqslant 1$. An offered prospect is strictly
> positive if its outcomes are all positive, ie if $x$, $y > 0$ and $p + q = 1$; it is strictly negative if its outcomes are all negative. A prospect is
> regular if it is neither strictly positive nor strictly negative.
> If $(x,p; y,q)$ is a regular prospect . . . then:
>
> (1) $V(x,p; y,q) = \pi(p)v(x) + \pi(q)v(y)$
>
> where $v(0) = 0$; $\pi(0) = 0$ and $\pi(1) = 1$ . . . $V$ is defined over prospects,
> while $v$ is defined on outcomes. The two scales coincide for sure prospects,
> where $V(x, 1.0) = V(x) = v(x)$ . . .
> The evaluation of strictly positive and strictly negative prospects are
> segregated into two components: (i) the riskless component, ie the
> minimum gain or loss which is certain to be obtained or paid; (ii) the
> risky component, ie the additional gain or loss which is actually at stake . . .
> If $p + q = 1$ and either $x > y > 0$ or $x < y < 0$, then
>
> (2) $V(x,p; y,q) = v(y) + \pi(p)[v(x) - v(y)]$.
>
> For example, $V(400,0.25; 100,0.75) = v(100) + \pi(0.25) [v(400) - v(100)]$ . . .
> Equation (2) reduces to equation (1) if $\pi(p) + \pi(1 - p) = 1$.
> . . . this condition is not generally satisfied. (Kahneman and Tversky
> 1979: 275–6).

The general form that Kahneman and Tversky suggest for the
weighting function, which provides subjective weights, with a sum
generally less than unity, is portrayed in Figure 7.1 (Figure 4 in
Kahneman–Tversky 1979: 283).

This specification is in accordance with the findings and suggestions of Edwards, mentioned previously. Also the conclusion drawn
from their empirical evidence concerning the value function, which
became a postulate in their Prospect Theory, that it differs for gains
and losses, is just an echo of the findings of Edwards:

> The results showed [the importance] in determining choices [of] general
> preferences or dislikes for risk-taking . . . subjects strongly preferred low
> probabilities of losing large amounts of money to high probabilities of
> losing small amounts of money – they just didn't like to lose (Edwards
> 1954a: 398).

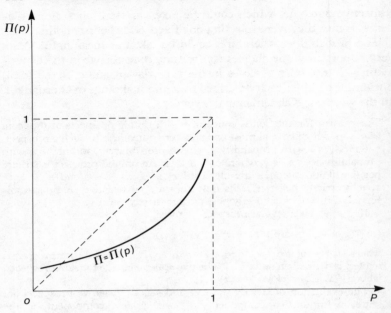

*Figure 7.1*

Kahneman and Tversky conclude:

> In the positive domain, the certainty effect contributes to a risk averse
> preference for a sure gain over a larger gain that is merely probable.
> In the negative domain, the same effect leads to a risk seeking preference
> for a loss that is merely probable over a smaller loss that is certain.
> The same psychological principle – the overweighting of certainty –
> favours risk aversion in the domain of gains and risk seeking in the
> domain of losses (Kahneman and Tversky 1979: 268-9).

Their suggested value function is similar to that illustrated in Figure
7.2 (ibid.: 279, Figure 3). This value function is familiar enough;
it has long been advocated by Markowitz (1959) in his extensive
analysis of choice under 'uncertainty' as applied to portfolio selection.

In Prospect Theory, however, to reiterate the point, the decision-
taker is never assumed to be confronted by a choice over gambles,
or prospects, which offer a mixture of gains and losses. The value
function might well be appropriate to such situations; but has never
been utilized to handle them. Likewise, to recapitulate, Regret
Theory, different though it is from Prospect Theory, has only been
explicated for the case of 'positive' or 'negative' prospects.

The use of Prospect Theory and Regret Theory has been limited

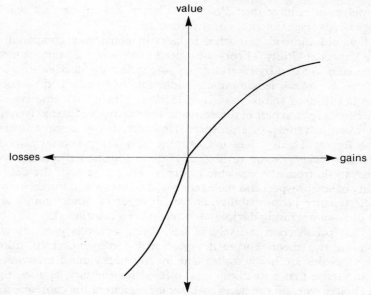

*Figure 7.2*

to narrowly specified gambles, so that the possibility of these theories being applied in the context of wider 'gambles', which can embrace choice of assets, is not that immediate. However, the brilliant paper by Machina (1982), which generalizes the kind of approach embedded in Prospect Theory, namely that the choice-index is non-linear in probabilities rather than linear as in Expected Utility, suggests that such a framework could handle wider issues, such as the selection of the best portfolio. However, it is not certain that the precise form of the framework used in Regret Theory *per se* is that versatile. The more readily versatile paradigm would seem to be Prospect Theory, but it is no more esoteric and perhaps less acceptable to intuition and introspection than Regret Theory. The version of Prospect Theory currently available possesses all of the limitations of the Expected Utility Theory; essentially, even if at one stage removed, it is founded on probability and it accepts a weighted average procedure over outcomes as a mechanism for epitomizing prospects.

Regret Theory also relies on probability as a measure of degree of belief in outcomes; and it employs the apposite probabilities as weights in the calculation of the individual's index of regret. Its principal advantage over Prospect Theory lies in the fact that it does not average outcomes over prospects.

I would contend that what it lacks in concinnity compared to the Expected Utility Theory, or indeed to Prospect Theory, is more than compensated by its endeavour to conflate the decision-making process by acknowledging that all outcomes in any defined prospect will not (indeed someone such as Herbert Simon or Heiner would say cannot) play a part in the derivation of the index of attractiveness, or unattractiveness, of a prospect. However, I would argue further that Regret Theory does not capture fully the process by which decision-makers do (or, turning this into a judgemental constatation, seem to do from the available evidence) epitomize both the desirability of any prospect and their ranking of all prospects. Furthermore, their reliance on probability as the conveyor of 'uncertainty', and its use as a weighting device, has already been mentioned.

That predilection is likely to have been a corollary of the fact that the two theories were designed with lottery tickets in mind. The theories are not accompanied by any background motivation, in the sense that a justification is offered for the tacit opinion that all choices wherein the decision-taker is nescient of the consequences of his selected strategy can be envisaged as mere extensions of fixed-odd bets. Decision-makers can find objective probability distributions for the 'uncertain' outcomes, and do so costlessly. There is no cognizance taken of the possibility either that objective probabilities might not be accessible, or that, as their replacement, subjective probabilities might be logically inconsistent with the modelling of choice under ignorance.

It is unlikely that decision-makers, certainly in an economic context, will find themselves in total ignorance of the outcomes of specified strategies (so that something like the Hurwicz index or the Arrow–Hurwicz (1972) optimality criterion would be appropriate). Nevertheless decision-makers will be in situations where, even if from historical data and future guesses at the unfolding of economic events they can place what they regard as realistic bounds on the range of outcomes of a given strategy, their knowledge will be incomplete. They might well imagine just several discrete outcomes could follow from, say, a particular investment decision such as to purchase a new machine. In the case of an entrepreneur considering the advantage of launching a new product line, the range of outcomes, of course, is also likely to be doubtful.

In addition, in cases such as that, as well as in more conventional, and less uncertain, decision-requiring situations, the individual will not have sufficient information to calculate probabilities. Inevitably, objective probabilities as relative frequencies, carrying the kind of time-variant knowledge that is supposed in decision-making models, do not exist. Of course, they can exist for economic agents wishing to take particular decisions; such as an insurance company seeking to determine the optimum premia it should charge for life insurance cover offered to individuals. The company can obtain reliable data on the health characteristics that prolong or reduce life for the population, so computing life-tables with probabilities that can meaningfully be applied to the sample of the population applying to it for life cover.

Savage (1954) has argued and claimed to have proved that objective probability can be replaced by subjective probability – with the latter having all of the properties of a distributional variable. In essence, all probabilities relating to the outcomes in any prospect must sum to unity; certainty of the occurrence of an individual outcome must be assigned a probability of unity; attaching a subjective probability of zero to any outcome means that it cannot occur. Leaving on one side the question as to the way that an individual might gather data together to form a view as to the feasible outcomes, and their chances of occurrence, for a defined strategy, even the assumption that decision-makers will be able to compute subjective probabilities is of questionable value, meaning and applicability to issues of choice of action under uncertainty.

Prospect Theory can account for the behaviour discovered through the numerous laboratory experiments on gambles, but, as I have reiterated, it relies on the probability approach and an averaging procedure to calculate the index that epitomizes the overall worth of any prospect. Regret Theory does not require that averaging process; it is more in line with introspection, but it is based upon probability and a form of expectation principle: and it is not compatible with all empirical evidence. Neither theory has yet been developed to analyse more complex and broader action-choices than those implied in choice of lottery tickets with only two non-zero outcomes.

# 8 Perspective Theory Versus Alternative Paradigms: A Summing Up and Suggestions for a Programme of Empirical Experimentation

The theory I have endeavoured to adumbrate in the preceding pages is one that can be seen as an *ex post facto* rationalization of the empirical evidence that has vitiated Expected Utility Theory. It was, however, designed in outline before it became clear that it would, quite readily, satisfy the demands imposed by that evidence. That is of no import *per se*; for theories such as Prospect Theory and Regret Theory were propounded precisely because they offered paradigms that would provide a rationalization of the experimental evidence.

In terms of models of decision-making in an uncertain environment, where the measure of uncertainty is encapsulated in probability, before Prospect Theory and Regret Theory were developed, only Hicks's 'three moment' theory of choice over probability distributions' could, so I have claimed (but not fully proved here by using the Safety-First models), determine choices in a way revealed by the empirical tests of Expected Utility Theory. The Hicksian Theory, despite its psychological appeal and its ready translation into every-day concepts (without the need for economic agents to have been steeped in statistical theory), is unconvincing because it does not satisfy (does not inevitably satisfy) the absolute preference or stochastic dominance axiom embedded in the Von Neumann–Morgenstern framework and accepted universally as the *sine qua non* of any worthwhile theory of decision-making under uncertainty.

In my view, Prospect and Regret Theories, whilst embodying some key features and being able to characterize the choices made by respondents in the empirical tests of Expected Utility Theory, do not capture the essence of choice under uncertainty. Nor do they extend their coverage readily to complex and broader action-choice problems in economics, of the kind discussed in Chapters 4 and

5 above. Additionally, they accept probability as the uncertainty-variable and rely upon an 'expectations' principle for guiding the individual decision-maker's choice of action.

The Hicks and Shackle approaches seem to capture the risk-averter's desire to use a measure of the spread of returns and their bunching towards the upper or lower end of the range, as indicators of the risk involved in any prospect; or indeed of the lower risk involved should there be a large positive skewness to outcomes. However, though Hicks is obviously correct in suggesting that what is being searched for is some kind of index that will epitomize uncertain prospects – bearing in mind some of the key characteristics of those prospects – his own index is not acceptable. Besides not being uniquely consistent with the stochastic dominance axiom, it also uses an 'averaging procedure' for outcomes (*ex hypothesi*) which means also that gains and losses are taken together, and, again as a corollary, it is not a theory that can be used with a non-distributional uncertainty-variable.

Also by construction, Shackle's theory cannot be employed to tackle choice of action problems that are formulated in probability terms (except possibly by using the Fordian/Shacklesque model of Ford 1983). As the only theory to date that acts as an antidote to the models founded on the probability calculus (save for the really non-comparable models of behaviour under complete ignorance) Shackle's theory is a veritable *tour de force*; a *magnum opus* of great originality. Yet, his uncertainty-variable is problematical; and the separate pillars of his construct do not always have clear and separate roles to play in the resolution of the best choice of action. Furthermore, it is not likely to be the case, except in special conditions, that Shackle's theory can explain multi-asset portfolio diversification. Shackle develops his theory on the assumption of what might be called strong risk-aversion, where losses are assessed separately from gains by the decision-taker; he never combines them. With that axiom of behaviour I agree; but Shackle never articulates his model for those situations where there are only gains or losses. We are left to infer that his model as formulated for gains and losses applies *mutatis mutandis* to those instances. In that case, even though Shackle's theory can solve for the optimal strategy for the individual to select, I would suggest that – just as in his theory for choices involving gains and losses, the individual balances, as it were, the 'best' against the 'worst' – he is also likely to do so in situations where the choices (say of lottery tickets) before him are for just losses: he weighs the worst loss against the 'best' loss for each and every lottery ticket. That is an hypothesis that might be right or wrong: and if wrong, Perspective Theory can account for the 'only gains' and 'only losses' lottery ticket choices described in Chapter 2 by the maximization of $\phi(.)$ or by the selection of the lottery tickets that leads to the lowest (maximum) value of $\psi(.)$.

Perspective Theory can preserve one of the essential features of Shackle's schema (the separation of gains from losses) and the central feature of Hicks's theory, also shared by Shackle's, namely that the 'best' and 'worst' features of uncertainty prospects figure prominently in the selection of the best action-choice. Perspective Theory can also be cast in terms of a non-distributional variable. It is also a theory that can solve for action-choices for a wide range of contexts and is consistent with the available experimental evidence.

Nevertheless I do not wish to claim too much. I have stated *passim* that I cannot expect that *a* theory of decision-making under uncertainty will be suited to all possible choice of action schemes, even within the confines of economics. Nevertheless, Perspective Theory does provide a versatile paradigm that can offer a potential competitor to existing theories. A straightforward yardstick by which to compare theories is this: a theory can be taken to be superior to any competing theory if it can explain the phenomena explained by a competing theory and at least one other phenomenon. On this 'Pareto superior' definition, I am not perhaps being too presumptuous if I claim an advantage for my theory, at this stage of its development, over Prospect Theory and Regret Theory; also over Hicks's 'three moment' theory and Shackle's 'potential-surprise' theory.

I can claim, indisputably, that Perspective Theory seems to have an even greater edge over Expected Utility Theory. Despite the variations on that probabilistic-based approach to modelling decisions under uncertainty, which have been proposed as replacements for it, Expected Utility Theory does still tend to dominate the literature and thought in this field of economics, as Machina (1982) pointed out (*see* page 1). Its elegance and especially its normative properties seem to win the day; the lack of verisimilitude of its positive implications seems to be discounted with great alacrity.

The Expected Utility Theory has been expounded for 250 years; and it would be good to think that Machina was incorrect in his judgement that the theory was set fair to continue as the predominant, even if not exclusive, paradigm that economists will utilize in the future to analyse decision-making under incomplete knowledge. There seem to be metaphysical reasons for accepting the theory's normative aspects and for so much prominence being attached to them. There is something like the Aristotelean philosophy that lies behind the faith in the intrinsic incontrovertibility of the axiomatic framework of the Expected Utility Theory. For example, before Newton's work on gravity, the Middle Ages thought of the phenomenon of falling bodies in Greek style: an apple falls downwards and not upwards because it is the nature of an apple to fall down.

Those who challenge the behavioural basis of the Expected Utility Theory, such as Herbert Simon (1982), do so because they believe that both the axioms and the positive conclusion (the empirical proposition epitomized in the Expected Utility Theorem) are erroneous. They do not accept the inexorable rightness of the theory, just because it has the allegedly desirable attribute of describing consistent, rational behaviour, which if it could be tested properly would be correct as a positive theory (because it is right by its very nature; the meta-theory argument).[1] Rather, the behaviourists challenge the assumption of the theory and its underlying thesis that individuals can and do make reasoned choices in situations of uncertainty. Individuals, they argue, do not have the ability to reason out their choices in the way described by the Expected Utility Theory; too much knowledge of logic, statistical theory, as well as access to a computer, is required. This viewpoint has similarities to those of other celebrated Greek philosophers: the Socratic argument reported in Plato's *Republic* that the populace will be unable to perceive justice if they do not know what justice is first of all; they must then be educated.

Against that kind of argument the retort can be the familiar one: it will suffice if an economic agent's choice of strategy can be explained by the particular set of behavioural postulates, so that it can assumed that he behaves 'as if' the postulates were correct. The 'as if' view can be pressed too hard; but it is a partial counter to the Simonesque position. However, in contrast to the meta-theory defence of Expected Utility Theory, it lays the emphasis on the positive attributes of any given theory.

That is the emphasis that I think is the more important. Yet, I do also hold the (non-Friedman 1953) opinion that the behavioural axioms of any theory should have credibility: but the central issue is whether or not the decision-rule that emerges from the theory does hold up to empirical evaluation. It is true that once a skeletal framework that purports to describe behaviour is formalized it can produce testable propositions that are deducible only by the individual with expertise and technical knowledge. This is true even of a theory such as George Shackle's, which is initially set out by him in 'descriptive' terms: once formalized it seems very sophisticated and to demand much mental gymnastics on behalf of the individual decision-maker.

Naturally, the same observation can be made from a study of Expected Utility Theory, Prospect Theory or Regret Theory. It is no less true of Perspective Theory; but there this only becomes noticeable over the question of portfolio choice, which is inherently a complex matter in any theory. The seeming difficulties materialize only when it is endeavoured to use the theory to the full. They do not occur if we suppose the question of the best portfolio to select is solved for a constrained, limited, set of alternative investments. This will probably be the case for small investors; and for some institutions this would be so because of the controls that regulate their behaviour. Then, furthermore, the choice of actual portfolio from the reduced-set, it is suggested, is accomplished by the procedures contained in the pillars of Perspective Theory, even if subconsciously, by the individual, and, even if not mathematically in the way I have demonstrated the matter, as the logic of complete formalization required.

Perspective Theory describes and systematizes a structure for decision-making under uncertainty. It attempts to actualize what appears to transpire in the psyche when decisions are being contemplated. It provides a series of logical steps by which the decision is effectively taken; on the 'as if' basis, it offers a formalization of the steps that are taken subconsciously as decisions are reached.

The foundation of the theory, as I have reiterated, is a belief that something like the mechanism I have propounded is consistent with psychological considerations; but although it does seem to have intuitive support, the theory at least has the experimental evidence to bolster it. In that regard it can always be seen as an endeavour to deduce a framework compatible with that evidence.

If the theory had been propounded solely to fit the laboratory evidence then that would have been an extremely narrow objective. It must be conceded that that evidence is a limited and very special type of evidence upon which to found a theory that has something to contribute not only to the analysis of decision-making over a wideish area but also to the analysis of decision-making under uncertainty (for a similar view, *see* Carter 1953).

There are, in effect, several drawbacks to the laboratory experiments conducted to evaluate axioms of choice and, *inter alia*, the Expected Utility Theory. The two major ones are as follows. The first is that the experiments involved probabilities, which were known to the participants, being stated on the gambles or bets. Even though the participants, on occasions, formed their subjective probabilities or decision-weights from the 'objective' probabilities, the experiments were never designed to seek out how subjects formulated uncertainty-variables. The second deficiency, a corollary of the first, is that the experiments were confined to simple choices over simple lottery tickets or bets. The subjects were not asked how they would formulate a solution to a particular action-choice problem. The infor-

mation they did provide about their behaviour under uncertainty
might not, therefore, reveal their true behaviour and attitudes; these
could have been suppressed by the constrained, and perhaps
contrived, choice-problems they were given to solve.

Once tests are designed to countervail those deficiencies, the crucial
lacunae that they have left will be filled. More will be known about
the nature of uncertainty-variables; the type of information economic
agents utilize; the extent of any editing of that information; and
it may be possible to extract the structure of the process they do
use in order to obtain a solution, even if they do not formulate
it rigorously. Of course, further tests that enabled that process to
be brought to the fore more overtly would be the ultimate, ideal,
test.

Such empirical research would be extensive by its very nature
and, if feasible, would need to encompass several varieties of
economic agents to incorporate different types of decision-making
situations. However, without it it is not possible to proceed very
far with an empirical assessment of models of choice under uncertainty; nor is it feasible to assess the value of competing theories.
Further research along the lines followed in the past thirty years'
testing for the axioms of Expected Utility Theory or of the Edwards–
Kahneman–Tversky (Machina) Prospect Theory will serve little purpose. Yet, until that further, broader, research is undertaken, I can
claim that Perspective Theory can explain the empirical evidence
(and the experimental research of J.G. Lynch (1978) supports my
notion of the ascendancy function), and it can be used to solve
a range of choice-problems; further, it is a theory that can accommodate a true uncertainty-variable. Those further empirical inquiries
might reveal that such a concept is not, indeed, a fanciful one.

## Notes

1 There is, however, even some doubt in the mind of philosophers about the empirical content of metaphysical statements. The great American philosopher, C.S.
Peirce, for example, claimed that: (i) 'Metaphysics seeks to give an account of
the universe of mind and matter ... it rests on phenomenology and on normative
science' (Hartshorne and Weiss 1931: 186); (ii) 'Its attitude towards the universe
is nearly that of the special sciences from which it is distinguished by confining
itself to such parts of physics and of psychics as can be established without
special means of observation. But these are very peculiar parts, extremely unlike
the rest' (ibid.: 282); and (iii) 'Metaphysics, even bad metaphysics, really rests
on observations, whether consciously or not; and the only reason that this is
not universally recognised is that it rests upon kinds of phenomena with which
every man's experience is so saturated that he usually pays no particular attention
to them' (Hartshorne and Weiss 1935: 2).

# References

Allais, M. (1953), 'Le comportement de l'homme rationnel devant le risque. Critique des postulates et axiomes de l'école americaine', *Econometrica*, 21, October, 503–46.

Arrow, K.J. and Hurwicz, L. (1972), 'An optimality criterion for decision making under ignorance', in C.F. Carter and J.L. Ford (eds), *Expectations and Uncertainty in Economics, Essays in honour of G.L.S. Shackle*, Oxford: Basil Blackwell, 1–11.

Arzac, E.R. (1976), 'Profits and safety in the theory of the firm under price uncertainty', *International Economic Review*, 17, February, 163–71.

Ayer, A.J. (1972), *Probability and Evidence*, London: Macmillan.

Bell, D.E. (1981), *Regret in Decision-making under Uncertainty*, Harvard Business School Working Paper, 82–15.

Bernouilli, D. (1738), 'Specimen theoriae novae de mensura sortis', *Commentarri Academiae Scientiarum Imperialis Petropolitanae*, V, 175–82. Translated by L. Sommer as 'Expositions of a new theory on the measurement of risk', *Econometrica*, 22, January, 23–36.

Block, M.K. and Heineke, H.M. (1973), 'The allocation of effort under uncertainty: the case of risk averse behaviour', *Journal of Political Economy*, March/April, 376–85.

Borch, K. (1974), 'The rationale of the mean–standard deviation analysis: comment', *American Economic Review*, 64, June, 428–50.

Carter, C.F. (1950), 'Expectation in economics', *Economic Journal*, 66, March, 92–105.

Carter, C.F. (1953), 'A revised theory of expectations', *Economic Journal*, 68, December, 428–50.

Carter, C.F. Meredith, G.P. and Shackle, G.L.S. (eds) (1954), *Uncertainty and Business Decisions*, Liverpool: Liverpool University Press.

Dorfman, R. (1955), Review of Carter, C.F. Meredith, G.P. and Shackle, G.L.S., (eds) (1954), *Uncertainty and Business Decisions*, Liverpool: Liverpool University Press, in *Review of Economics and Statistics*, 37, August.

Dreze, J. and Modigliani, F. (1972), 'Consumption decisions under uncertainty', *Journal of Economic Theory*, 5, 308–35.

Dreze, J. (1974), 'Axiomatic theories of choice, cardinal utility and subjective probability', in his *Allocation under Uncertainty: Equilibrium and Optimality*, New York: Wiley, 1–23.

Edwards, W. (1953), 'Probability-preferences in gambling', *American Journal of Psychology*, 66, 349–64.

Edwards, W. (1954a), 'Probability preferences among bets with differing expected values', *American Journal of Psychology*, 67, 55–67.

Edwards, W. (1954b), 'Variance preference in gambling', *American Journal of Psychology*, 67, 441–52.

Edwards, W. (1954c), 'The theory of decision making', *Psychological Bulletin*, 51, no. 4, 380–417.

Edwards, W. (1955), 'The prediction of decisions among bets', *Journal of Experimental Psychology*, 50, 201–14.

Egerton, R.A.D. (1960), *Investment Decisions Under Uncertainty*, Liverpool: Liverpool University Press.

Fishburn, P.C. (1981), 'Nontransitive Measurable Utility', Bell Laboratory Economics Discussion Paper, 209.

Fishburn, P.C. and Kochenberger, G.A. (1982), 'Two-piece Von Neumann–Morgenstern utility functions', mimeographed; cited in Kahneman and Tversky (1979).

Ford, J.L. (1983), *Choice, Expectation and Uncertainty*, Oxford: Basil Blackwell.

Ford, J.L. (1985), 'Shackle's theory of decision making under uncertainty: synopsis and brief appraisal', *Journal of Economic Studies*, 12, no. 1/2, 1985, Special Issue on the Economics of G.L.S. Shackle, 49–69.

Friedman, M. (1953), *Essays in Positive Economics*, Chicago: Chicago University Press.

Hartshorne, C. and Weiss, P. (1931), *The Collected Papers of Charles Peirce*, I, Cambridge, Mass: Harvard University Press.

Hartshorne, C. and Weiss, P. (1935), VI, Cambridge, Mass: Harvard University Press.

Heiner, R.A. (1983), 'The origin of predictable behaviour', *American Economic Review*, 73, December, 560–95.

Hicks, J.R. and Allen, R.G.D. (1934), 'A reconsideration of the theory of value', *Economica*, NS1, February, 52–76, and May, 196–219.

Hicks, J.R. (1935) 'A suggestion for simplifying the theory of money', *Economica*, NS2, February, 1–19.

Hicks, J.R. (1967), *Critical Essays in Monetary Theory*, Oxford: The Clarendon Press.

Hicks, J.R. (1977), *Economic Perspectives*, Oxford: The Clarendon Press.

Hurwicz, L. (1951), 'Optimality criteria for decision making under uncertainty', Cowles Commission Discussion Paper.

Jeffreys, H. (1939), *Theory of Probability* (1st edn), Oxford: Oxford University Press.

Kahneman, D.H. and Tversky, A. (1979), 'Prospect theory: an analysis of decision under risk', *Econometrica*, 47, March, 263–91.

Kataoka, S. (1963), 'A stochastic programming model', *Econometrica*, 21, January–April, 181–96.

Keynes, J.M. (1921), *Treatise on Probability*, London: Macmillan.

Kunreuther, H.R. *et al.* (1978), *Disaster Insurance Protection: Public Policy Lessons*, New York: Wiley.

Loomes, G. and Sugden, R. (1982), 'Regret theory: an alternative theory of rational choice under uncertainty', *Economic Journal*, 92, December, 805–24.

Luce, D. and Raiffa, H. (1957), *Games and Decisions*, New York: John Wiley.

Lynch, J.G. Jnr (1979), 'Why additive utility models fail as descriptions of choice behaviour', *Journal of Experimental Social Psychology*, 15, 397–417.

Machina, M. (1982), ' "Expected utility" analysis without the independence axiom', *Econometrica*, 50, March, 277–323.

Markowitz, H. (1952), 'Portfolio selection', *Journal of Finance*, 7, March, 77–91.

Markowitz, H. (1959), *Portfolio Selection*, New York: Wiley.

Mosteller, F. and Magee, P. (1951), 'An experimental measurement of utility', *Journal of Political Economy*, 55, 371–404.

Peirce, C.S. (1949), *Chance, Love and Logic*, a collection of his essays edited by M.R. Cohen, New York: Peter Smith.

Pratt, J.W. (1964), 'Risk aversion in the small and in the large', *Econometrica*, 32, 122–36.

Preston, M.G. and Baratta, P. (1948), 'An experimental study of the auction-value of an uncertain outcome', *American Journal of Psychology*, 61, 183–93.

Pyle, D.H. and Turnovsky, S.J. (1970), 'Safety-first and expected utility maximisation in mean–standard deviation portfolio analysis', *Review of Economics and Statistics*, 52, 75–81.

Roy, A.D. (1952), 'Safety-first and the holding of assets', *Econometrica*, 20, July, 431–49.

Samuelson, P.A. (1963), 'Discussion: problems of methodology', *American Economic Review Proceedings*, 53, May, 231–6.

Sandmo, A. (1970), 'The effect of uncertainty on saving decisions', *Review of Economic Studies*, 37, 353–60.

Sandmo, A. (1971), 'On the theory of the competitive firm under price uncertainty', *American Economic Review*, 61, March, 65–73.

Savage, L.J. (1951), 'The theory of statistical decision', *Journal of* the *American Statistical Association*, 46, 55–67.

Savage, L.J. (1954), *The Foundation of Statistics*, New York: Wiley.

Schoemaker, P.J.H. (1982), 'The expected utility model: its variants, purposes, evidence and limitations', *Journal of Economic Literature*, 20, June, 529–63.

Shackle, G.L.S. (1952), *Expectation in Economics* (2nd edn), Cambridge: Cambridge University Press.

Shackle, G.L.S. (1961), *Decision, Order and Time in Human Affairs*, (1st edn), Cambridge: Cambridge University Press.

Simon, H.A. (1963), 'Discussion: problems of methodology', *American Economic Review Proceedings*, 53, May, 229–31.

Simon, H.A. (1979), 'Rational decision making in business organisation', *American Economic Review*, 69, September, 493–513.

Simon, H.A. (1982), *Reason in Human Affairs*, Oxford: Basil Blackwell.

Telser, L.G. (1955-56), 'Safety-first and hedging', *Review of Economic Studies*, 23, February, 1–16.

Tobin, J. (1958), 'Liquidity preference as behaviour toward risk', *Review of Economic Studies*, 25, February, 65–86.

Tsiang, S.C. (1972), 'The rationale of the mean–standard deviation analysis, skewness preference and the demand for money', *American Economic Review*, 62, June, 345–71.

Tversky, A. and Kahneman, D. (1974), 'Judgement under uncertainty: heuristics and biases', *Science*, 185, 1124–31.

Von Neumann, J. and Morgenstern, O. (1944, 1947), *The Theory of Games and Economic Behaviour*, Princeton: Princeton University Press (first edn, 1944; second edn, 1947).

Williams, A.C. (1966), 'Attitudes towards speculative risks as an indicator of attitudes toward pure risks', *Journal of Risk and Insurance*, 33, 577–86.

# Index

empiricism *see* experiments
Engel Aggregation, 55, 64, 67
expectation principle, 11
  *see also* Prospect Theory and
    Regret Theory
'expectation' principle, 26
Expected Utility Theory and
    Theorem, vii–viii, 1–26, 41,
    132–7
  axioms of, 2, 14–16, 42, 125:
    inconsistency with, 18–20
  decision criteria under
    uncertainty, 1–13
  empirical investigation *see*
    experiments
  and 'microeconomics of
    uncertainty', 73, 79, 80, 84 86,
    90, 92n
  portfolio selection, 47–8, 73
  and Prospect Theory and Regret
    Theory, 123–6
expected value, 26
experiments
  Expected Utility Theory and
    Theorem, 3–4, 8, 11, 17–26,
    136–7
  Perspective Theory, 29, 33
  Prospect Theory and Regret
    Theory, 123–31
  suggested, 132–7

finances *see* portfolio selection
financial institutions, 13, 29, 30
firms, 13, 73
  perfectly competitive, output
    choice for, 73, 84–9
Fishburn, P.C., 21, 125
Ford, J.L., ix, 10, 14, 73, 95, 101,
    102, 104–6, 108, 133
Friedman, M., 4

gain and loss elements, 12, 31–9
  *see also* ascendancy index and
    function; portfolio selection;
    risk aversion; Shackle, theory
gambling experiments, 108
  *see also* experiments

Hartshorne, C., 137n
Heineke, H.M., 80

Heiner, R.A., 23, 24, 72, 130
Hicks, Sir J.R., 1, 12, 22–3, 25 41,
    65, 101, 132–4
  *see also* mean/variance theory
Hurwicz, L., 130

independence axiom of Expected
    Utility Theory, 18–20
index
  of credibility *see* degree of belief/
    credibility index
  Perspective, 31–2
inductive theory *see* Prospect
    Theory and Regret Theory
inflation assumed to be non-
    existent, 47
investment
  in real capital, 73, 89–92
  *see also* portfolio selection
irrelevance of independent
    alternatives: axiom of
    Expected Utility Theory 15

Jeffreys, H., 8

Kahneman, D.H., 4, 11, 17–21, 24,
    109, 125–8, 137
Kataoka, S., 12
Keynes, J.M., 8, 29
Knight, F., vii
Kochenberger, G.A. 21
Kunreuther, H.R., 4

laboratory experiments *see*
    experiments
labour choice model in Perspective
    Theory, 73, 80–4
Loomes, G., 11, 124–5
loss *see* gain and loss elements
lottery *see* gambling experiments
Luce, D., 14
Lynch, J.G., 137

Machina, M., 1, 2, 6, 11, 21, 129,
    134, 137
Magee, P., 3
Marginal Advantage, 64–5
Markowitz, H., 12, 14, 17, 21, 22,
    128
  *see also* mean/variance theory